SOULED OUT:

COMBAT PTSD

A MEMOIR OF WAR
AND INNER PEACE

MICHAEL S. ORBAN

Souled Out: A Memoir of War and Inner Peace

Published by
Minuteman Press
1423 W. Washington Street
West Bend, WI 53095
262-338-2223
www.westbend.minutemanpress.com

Second Edition February 2011
Revised Edition March 2014

Library of Congress Control Number: 2007927646
ISBN-13: 978-0-9767581-1-2
ISBN-10: 0-9767581-1-3

Book Cover and Interior design by Phil Olson / baddog creative
Edited by MariJo Moore

Printed in the United States of America

"Michael Orban served as a 20-year-old infantry soldier in Vietnam and in his superbly written autobiography *Souled Out: A Memoir Of War And Inner Peace* takes the reader along on his journey through a disastrous war and into his experiences of loneliness, emptiness, spiritual scarring and psychological destruction. The underlying message of *Souled Out* is that the psychological wounds of war are as serious as the physical ones and can be remedied and recovered from, and that there is relief for and from them."

-*Midwest Book Review*

"Having read quite a few books on PTSD, I believe Michael Orban definitely conveys the feelings and thoughts that I have experienced and live with on a daily basis in his book *Souled Out*; none of the other books come close to this one. Having been a Combat Medic in the "Bloody Red One" in Vietnam in 66-67, and living with these feelings for over 40 years, it is time to give our combat troops all the help they need."

- Mike Maure, Combat Medic
  1st Infantry Division, Vietnam 66-67

"I read Mike's book after it was recommended to me by a respected counselor at the VA. The book is an adventure story with a message. There isn't any preaching or psycho babble. What you get is one veteran's story of attempting to deal with the horrors of combat. Mike found his way home by first seeking immersion in the jungles of Africa. I found my way by first getting lost in the catacomb of libraries at my law school. We come home empty, confused, and disconnected with a desire to find our way into a new identity. At some point, we emerge from the darkness. Mike's book, radio show, and personal friendship have been a road map for me to move forward from my war trauma. I recommend his book to all warriors as a wonderful stepping stone towards healing and enlightenment.

- SGT Will Parzyszek (U.S. Army, Retired)
  Iraq War Combat Veteran
  Wounded Warrior

"Michael has dove deep into PTSD with a side of compassion that reaches the souls of veterans exposed to the travesties of war. His writing also enlightens others to the torment and suffering that PTSD causes. The joinery in Mike's memoirs helps settle the inner peace to healing and overcoming the constant ritual of PTSD in daily life. Can't wait for the next one, Mike. Keep Us Healing!"

- EO1 Jeff Starke USN (SW)
  Retired 2005, 24 years service.
  Vietnam 1972-1975, Panama Invasion, Desert Shield, Desert Storm, (Presidential Recall) *Bombing of the World Trade Center 9-11,* Operation Enduring Freedom, Operation Iraqi Freedom II. Assigned to: Mobile Inshore Undersea Warfare unit (MIUWU) Team II

"This story will touch you whether you are a veteran or someone who wants to understand the path combat veterans walk."

- Jon Christensen, Vietnam, 67-68
  Milwaukee Vets Center
  Readjustment Counseling Therapist
  MSed, MS, LPC, CSAC, CRC

"I found this to be one of the most thought provoking books I have recently read. The experiences of Michael Orban in Vietnam and Africa are a wonderful adventure story, but also carry a powerful message about the impact war has on a soldier when placed back into civilian life. The descriptions of his struggles with Post Traumatic Stress Syndrome are so timely with the ongoing wars in Afghanistan and Iraq. The physical and emotional damage these conflicts are inflicting on our most patriotic men and women are painfully illustrated by Orban's experiences."

- Al Goshaw, Professor
  Duke University, NC

Mike's book, Souled Out, has helped many veterans that I work with. In a recent program graduation ceremony one of my veterans chose to use several paragraphs from the book as his "words of wisdom" to the group on his final day in the PTSD Program. Two other vets that I work with, (one served in Vietnam and one served in Iraq), heard Mike speak at a recent workshop and felt he inspired them to seek help in order to finally find some peace in their lives.

Deb Pergande
Trauma Specialist at VA Medical Center
Tomah, Wisconsin
February 2014

*For all those who, because of a traumatic experience,
are in that void of spiritual darkness, and are fighting
the battles to calm that inner place called a soul.*

CONTENTS

ACKNOWLEDGMENTS

First and foremost I am grateful to have known Loraine Rose Lofy – a woman who, because of divorce, was left alone to raise her ten children. The catastrophic failure of her religion and church to give her support and guidance devastated her. The death of a son in the prime of his life was a suffering only she knew. Yet, by example, she never surrendered her character and continually stayed in control of her soul. Able to laugh when I cried for her situation, she remains one of the finest human beings life has shared with me. She showed me that it is not whether you are male or female, it is the size of your character and devotion to the truth inside you that matters. I am also deeply proud to call this woman "Ma."

I offer heartfelt thanks and am deeply grateful for the following:

To my sister Peg and her family, my brother Tom and his family – without their help, I could not be here writing this. For all the life experiences that come from having five sisters and four brothers.

To Linda Vaughn Knief, former director of the Vietnam Veterans Memorial in Angel Fire, New Mexico, and the greatest representative of the Good Lord here on earth, who gave endless hours to me in spiritual guidance. Her dedication to the Vietnam Veteran has been soulful. She too paid a price to understand us.

To Dr. Jeffrey Durbin, Deb Pergande, the staff of the PTSD program at the Veterans Hospital in Tomah, Wisconsin, and the Veterans Administration in general for all the dedication given to better understand and advance the treatment of PTSD.

To Dr. Patti Levin for permission to reprint her "Trauma Response and Coping Skills" and her work with those who suffer from trauma.

To Elaine Pagels, Professor of Theology at Princeton University, whose insights were especially helpful in my search for spiritual awareness.

To Sharon Mitchell, teacher in West Bend, Wisconsin, who volunteered her time and skills to provide much help in the preliminary editing of this book.

To Diane Montgomery and Dyson Hunt, dear friends, for all their encouragement and support along the way.

To the people of the continent of Africa, especially the folks in Lebangy, Gabon, and the humble Pygmies for what they taught me.

To Dr. Albert Schweitzer and Mark Twain for what they gave and I received.

To the North Carolina Writers Network where I learned so much and feel so at home with others who seek through writing to express themselves and inspire each other. I am also thankful to them for introducing me to MariJo Moore, author/poet/editor/essayist. No one would be reading these words if she had not honored me by undertaking the editing of my manuscript. Her dedication, tireless effort, attention to detail and organizational skills are all woven into this work.

INTRODUCTION

My purpose in writing this book is to share my personal experiences and continuing battle with Post Traumatic Stress Syndrome with those who have had, or will have, a similar reaction to a traumatic event, as well as with their families and friends. Whether from war, personal tragedy, rape, abuse or other violence, the lasting effects of these harrowing ordeals need our attention. Our society can, and should, better understand and offer expedient emotional and spiritual relief for souls and minds so deeply wounded.

Even though my own traumatic experience came from the Vietnam War, I do not have a particular interest in that war, nor its history, battles, strategies or politics; all of these are for others. I have no interest in telling war stories, but am including several descriptions of events for the sake of helping you to visualize what I experienced, and the cause of the trauma that took me through years of hiding deep in the jungles of Central Africa.

Later, I wandered for thirty years like a nomad to almost every state in the US, across Canada, the Caribbean Islands, and Europe, trying desperately to keep my torment hidden behind the emotional shield I had developed to protect my sanity. Most of this wandering was a futile effort to escape what my mind could not understand or accept. But, no matter where I went and how far I ran, the one person I could not shake or outrun was myself.

I eventually confronted the haunting, eroded emotions and I had one of two choices: I could stop, face myself, and examine what was perilously hidden behind the protective, fortified barriers of my mind – the facade, the brick wall; or I could choose oblivion. The second choice, suicide, fought to be heard; it became almost a friend, no longer a fear. I knew that, if the mental torment got too bad, suicide was there to end it.

In the first part of the book I will discuss how I finally broke through to understand what was going on. I also offer thoughts on how things could be different both for the veteran and the country he or she served. We can and must do better for those who have sacrificed for us.

When I first realized, that more Vietnam Veterans died by suicide than died in the war, I was shocked. I read a retired VA doctor's estimate that from twenty thousand to over one hundred and fifty thousand people have taken their lives after returning from this war. But these numbers, always rounded to the nearest thousand, are not as daunting to me as the suicide committed by a man who had stood next to me in flesh, blood, and spirit.

One of my best friends from high school was on Firebase Maryann in Vietnam, in 1971, when the North Vietnamese Army overran the base, resulting in one of the bloodiest battles of the war. He was twenty-one years old.

With this book, I offer tribute to my friend who suffered more trauma than he could handle. He recounted his torment to me; later he put a gun to his head to end the suffering.

For many others as well, it is not about the numbers, but a specific loved one. Imagine the day-to-day, night-to-night emotional torment those people suffered (perhaps for years) before deciding they could endure no more. And what of the mothers, fathers, wives, sons, daughters and friends who have endured those crushing years and tragedies? They are victims of the war as well. Numerous people still cope with this daily.

The final incentive for me to bring my story forward came as the result of a simple phone call to my construction company requesting an estimate for repairs to a house. When I arrived, the owner of the house showed me the repairs he wanted. He somberly explained that his wife of more than forty years had passed; his sad voice seemed to imply it was time to move on. The easy estimate was reviewed and accepted and we arranged a day to begin work. I suggested a Thursday that drew the response, "No, I will be at the veterans hospital that day."

"Oh, you're a veteran," I said in the proud spirit generally offered between vets. "So am I! Which war?"

"Korea," he answered. No sooner had the word left his lips than his eyes filled with tears, and then he began crying. My heart ached for him. Estimates and home repairs forgotten, he motioned me to follow him to another room. Sobbing deeply, he pointed to a small shrine he had erected – a memorial to a war more than fifty years past. While my eyes took in the map on the wall of Korea and the display of service medals on a small wooden table beneath it, he began his story. "I was a combat medic in Korea in charge of twelve other combat medics. I was the only one to come home." That is all he said and all he needed to say; he could only cry more now. I felt compelled to hug him and did. I was filled with compassion for this man, and also enormous anger for those who had caused this suffering. He went on to say he had been receiving weekly counseling at the V.A. Hospital for eleven years! I stared at this man, who by all appearances looked like the average guy on the street. "I did the drinking thing," he added. Here was a man who had to be about seventy years old and was obviously deeply scarred by an activity over fifty years ago.

Later, I would think of the many stories I had heard of WWII vets and their families who spoke of this same hidden suffering from over sixty years ago; the hidden drinking, pacing floors in the middle of the night, nightmares and more. And all of these were men and women who had faced their military duties with honor. These were soldiers who had no shame to hide, only the burden of carrying the fact that they had performed the duties their country asked of them.

I realized this trauma was not just from the Vietnam War, but all wars! I knew I needed to write about this if for no other reason than to honor those who still suffer; to let them know it is OK and normal to have these reactions to war; that these feelings need not be hidden in alcohol, anger, anxiety and lonely walks down dark hallways at night. And as a way to give open support to families, letting them know it is OK to talk about their concerns and not an embarrassment to be hidden away in misery.

The term "Post Traumatic Stress" was not known to me until I was diagnosed with it in 1992, twenty years after the cause of my trauma. My story is of the long-term effects of trauma, and how the trauma was resolved to become a manageable scar.

It is important to me that you understand, especially after having lived in many countries, that I respect the U.S. Military, and the importance of maintaining a strong military force. The military provides many services around the world, besides handling combat and war: There are many different jobs in the military. But to me, the unique aspect of the psychology of the infantry solider is that he exists for one goal only: to kill the enemy. His is not a supporting role, helping others, as are many military jobs. I actually might have enjoyed making the military a career if I had not met that decision at a time in history when the military was in great transformation, responding to huge social changes from the prevailing attitudes of WWII to those of the sixties. At the peak of these alterations, a controversial war seemed to be both the cause of these changes, and conversely, the result of them.

The greatest effects on the military appeared to be expressed in racial and drug-related problems, along with decaying morale. I was especially disappointed and dismayed by the deep distrust, lack of respect, and even murder between officers and enlisted men. Yes, this actually happened, but this is not what history books have revealed. Witnessing all of this destroyed any chance I would have making the military a career.

In regard to the Vietnam War, in particular, I have heard every possible explanation, excuse, rationalization, views of the treatments of returning vets, protestors, those who fled to Canada, etc. Though all contain truths, they were not critical issues in the trauma that I experienced. Did these anger me? Yes, but they were not the cause of my trauma, instead they were side issues. There was something else, something internal that I just did not understand at the time. Years of wandering and finally meeting with one important man helped me understand the issues that ravaged my soul and then start to resolve them.

I realize that for each man who goes to war, there are as many different views of experiences. The guy right next to me in combat might have had a completely different reaction to battle than the one I had. I have met war veterans with a broad range of views, from those who still want to return to finish the war and avenge those who died, to those who put down their weapons but continued to "hump the boonies," while refusing to kill anyone, on any side.

Lastly, it is my conviction that lack of fear in combat is an irrational idea: Courage is simply refusing to let fear control your actions. In the environment of combat, the survival instinct arises and expresses itself as rage. Later I admitted it scared me to know that I had this rage inside, and may, as a result of my religious and social training, have been ashamed of it. Today I accept this instinctual rage as a factor of "life survival": the will to live being one of—or the most powerful—emotions

My experiences have been human. I now express the true feelings behind the rigid but brittle surface that hides rage. Of course, I know that as quickly as one can flick on a light switch these survival reactions can resurface. Although I don't like knowing that rage is part of me, in a raw way I am grateful to have felt the survival instinct many pretend is not there. I accept this instinct in myself and must be grateful, for I did survive.

I am not a psychologist. I only want to share my experiences with Post Traumatic Stress Syndrome in hopes they can help those of you who know its torment and suffering; those who understand what this syndrome steals. Then we can lead a happier and more spiritually fulfilled life.

West Bend, Wisconsin
November 2006

PART ONE:
WAR, ENDURANCE, AND THE
RETURN HOME

*Yea, though I walk through the valley of the shadow of death,
I will fear no evil, for I am the meanest Mother Fucker in the
valley!*

This, an infantry soldier's own version of the 23rd Psalm as he
walked through the jungle of Vietnam, is a perfect example of the
hardness, the raging reactionary persona of the fighting soldier.
I know because I was there with him in the same platoon. We
had to use this type of heresy to remain ruthless in the hell of
war: We wanted to live whether God was there or not. Upon
arrival in the Central Highlands, I was told from other soldiers
that the life expectancy of an infantry soldier was less than a
week. My tour of duty was an incomprehensible eternity that
lasted eleven months, seventeen days, and eighteen hours. Then,
like flying out of a nightmare, I left the jungle of Vietnam and
returned home to Wisconsin.

In Part One I want to explain how a boy filled with hopes and
dreams can go to war and a man with a soul filled with black
rage and fear can return. Without understanding something of
that you can't understand my story.

A FATAL PROMISE!

CHAPTER ONE

"I will never think of this again," I told myself as I ritualistically incinerated my dress green Army uniform in the basement of my house – coat, hat, pants, shoes, socks, medals, braided blue infantry rope: the whole ugly uniform. I watched the pieces disintegrate into ashes, then went upstairs convinced I could forget the insanity of war. I had lived nineteen years as a happy person, plagued only by petty grievances with my parents that amounted to nothing more than their love to properly guide and discipline me. I had loved to be outdoors, mostly near or in the river, passing my time in the woods building forts, fascinated by the wildlife of painted turtles, tiger frogs, muskrats, and dragonflies hovering over the water then darting off to other interests. I had felt the urge of a boy to have a crush on the neighbor girl and then drifted off to sleep with these new thoughts, and desires. My conscious world was limited to a few miles of home. Within less than two years I became a soul of darkness filled only with hatred, anger, shame, guilt and revenge. I no longer saw the beauty and fascination of life and it seemed to exist nowhere inside. Coming home had seemed like a promise of freedom. What I did not realize then, but would come to understand over the next thirty years, is what a great deception that promise would become.

The cold, hard, heavily reinforced mental defense system built with each day's experiences of the deadly dangers and horrific scenes of war was now so profoundly necessary that it would become a deeply rooted part of me. The realities of my youth and belief system were obliterated, and had no power to restore me when I returned from war. Trying to forget, trying desperately to block out those memories of war rather than acknowledge them, would eventually take all my energies. It would have the effect of putting those thoughts of fear, hatred, guilt, anger and shame, into a pressure cooker, locking the lid and setting the burner on high. Over the years these emotions would grow and rumble in that pressure cooker until steam whistled at its seams and it rattled violently on the burner, threatening to explode. I would find myself holding down the lid desperate to keep those emotions contained, afraid that if they got out I would travel into an insanity from which I would not return.

Intuitively I knew that I could not confront the intrusive memories from war; my mind had no way to deal with those experiences. I could not rationalize away the feelings, so they petrified and overwhelmed my reality. Upon returning from war, my life experience and knowledge could not pair up those experiences and feelings with any kind of understanding from which to draw answers. My upbringing had provided no preparations for the realities of war. The cold mental shield I had developed in combat to survive and protect the loving, compassionate and gentler emotions of my youth would have to stay in place and be vigilantly guarded. The lessons of war were not superficial but branded in my mind as the searing on the hide of cattle. The shield, the strong facade I presented, was what the world would see. It made me cold and hard, but did its job to hold back the tears, heartbreak, fear and anger. It kept me from crumbling to my knees, and helped me seem to survive on an outer level.

I was a soldier. Men had been going off to war for as long as there had been men. History books had shown us the glorious pictures of Charlemagne, Napoleon, Caesar, Civil War charges, World Wars I and II, and many more. They were all going off to war beautifully dressed, horses meticulously manicured, banners flying, breast armor polished and brilliant, reeking of courage and bravery; all heroes. Why did I not have those qualities? The deception of history books and historians would later become apparent and maddening regarding previous wars. No, I didn't seem to have those qualities, but I knew one thing: when I got home, no one, family nor friend nor society, would see the shattered soul. The steel shield would fabricate a mask, an exterior presence that I thought they needed to see, and one that would show me to be as history had pictured past soldiers. I would be the person my family and friends had known two years earlier. I would present my "heroic" image and maintain it. This determination shattered my soul into even more pieces. I learned quickly that memories have a way of remembering themselves, whether or not I voluntarily bring them to the surface. Although it is not my intention to elaborate on warfare - my interest centers on those who suffer PTSD, the emotional reaction and effects after a traumatic event - I will describe a few experiences to explain some of the images that triggered my own PTSD reactions.

Serving in an infantry division during the Vietnam War, I had gotten to know the jungle with its great and fascinating beauty of wild life and floral mysteries. Consequently, I also learned of the savagery, fear and panic that men created. I heard the yells and screams of terror during combat, and I saw the tranquility of the jungle exploding in machine gun fire, hand grenades and helicopter gun ships. I learned to be deeply grateful to the helicopter pilots and door gunners who heroically re-supplied us as they were hovering over firefights at night, kicking out boxes of ammunition through the jungle tree tops, exposing themselves to a barrage of bullets. I witnessed the cobra helicopter gun ships and pilots courageously bringing their incredible machines, not only lifting our morale, but also giving us such great advantage to stay alive. The jet fighter pilots and their spotters saved us in different ways while exposing themselves to destruction as well. And, of course, the medical pilots and crews could never have enough praise. All of these gutsy souls supported us infantry by giving protection, medicine, food, water, clean clothes, mail and more.

Chiseled in my mind's eye is an event that took place when I was on a forward firebase. Built by engineers, these bases were small areas of the jungle cleared of every living sprig of green growth, leaving only barren clay. Bulldozers pushed the dirt away from the center to form an earthen wall 4 or 5 feet high. Outside this dirt wall they cleared a good distance further to eliminate easy hiding and attack by our clever opponents. This open area protected the firebase using barbed wire and electric claymore mines. Inside the perimeter wall were placed the guns of the artillery and mortar crews along with the command bunker, field hospital, and mess area. And finally, for defense of these positions, small bunkers, about 12 feet long made of semi-circular corrugated steel and covered in sand bags. These circled the base just inside the perimeter wall. With an opening at each end for infantry soldiers, these provided shelters that any rodent would be proud of, but got poor ratings from humans. During the monsoon when these bases and bunkers turned to filthy slop, there was no end to the misery.

The purpose of these bases was primarily artillery and mortar support fire for soldiers out in the bush. As infantry soldiers we rotated out of the jungle every twelve to fifteen days to spend three days in defense of these small islands of desolation surrounded by the lush, beautiful jungle in which our adversaries were hiding. Once I was in the perfect blackness of night sitting on top of my assigned bunker. With noise kept to a minimum and even the light from a cigarette shielded from night and enemy, life seemed almost calm with only the stars to keep me company.

I was peering into the darkness, lost in thought, when the world exploded. Fireballs began shooting out of both ends of a nearby bunker illuminating everything and everyone on that side of the base. The thunderous explosion shook the ground horrifically. "What the fuck?" I screamed. Soldiers raced for weapons as confusion and shrieks replaced the tranquility. Were we under attack? Being overrun by the enemy? Then, just as quickly as the calm had been disturbed, the night returned to its blackness.

Suspecting we were under attack, the distinct metallic sound of rifle bolts slamming forward to firing position immediately filled the air, along with the thud of mortar tubes firing illumination rounds into the sky to expose the base. But in that eerie dull light, nothing was exposed. Nothing was out there! Nothing! Not one rifle was fired; there was nothing to fire at! Confused, wondering, and listening to voices screaming from near the attacked bunker, we waited cautiously for word of what was going on. I don't know how much time passed before the distinct whop, whop of helicopter blades came out of the night, then filled the air above us as they arrived at the base. There was no attack! It was a fragging! I had heard of these but had yet to witness one. A fragging was the intentional killing of American-by-American, usually by officers against lower echelon troops or vice versa. Seldom, if ever, did an officer above the rank of captain go out into the jungle with the infantry. It was commonly known that for officers the war was not worth losing their own lives, nor worth the medals, but worth keeping up the façade of honor to send others out to die.

As the helicopter landed to evacuate a fragging's latest victim, I kept my position on my bunker and was sickened to my soul when told the explosion was a claymore mine intentionally set off to kill the soldier in that bunker. I did not need to be told there was nothing that could live or even be recognizable after that blast. I don't know why the killing had been executed except that something had passed between the soldier and an officer: a threat, an insubordination, something serious or threatening.

I lost much respect for the military that night, and the truth of war not written in history books became a heartbreaking lesson. To this day, if a veteran tells me he was an infantry officer above the rank of captain in Vietnam, I can't help but look at him from many angles.

Another event that comes back to haunt me happened in the early morning haze and sweltering heat of the jungle the day after a ferocious late afternoon and nighttime battle with the Vietcong. Both armies on the move, we walked into Them. The quiet, typical hand signals and whisperings of communication were replaced by the explosion of screaming, frightened Vietnamese voices. It was spine chilling to hear those foreign screams erupting through the quiet of the jungle. There was a rapid succession of demands for their surrender, a refusal, and then the madness of machine gun fire. We were all engaged.

My job as an assistant machine gunner was to run around collecting the boxes of belted ammo for the "big gun" that other soldiers carried, along with the clips of ammo for their personal weapons. Before battle I had pictured myself running from soldier to soldier, collecting the metal boxes of ammo, running back to link the belts up and feed them into the M-60 machine gun. It didn't happen quite as I had imagined. There was massive gunfire from all directions. I scrabbled as low to the ground as I could get, grabbed the boxes and threw them back in the general direction of the big gun. Suddenly, I heard someone yelling that I had been hit. Mentally I went through a quick check of my body. Hit! Hit where? Is this what it feels like? Why can't I feel blood running or the pain of a wound? Was I paralyzed? All of these questions occurred in a flash of thought. But I felt nothing and would later find I had been hit in my favorite can of C-ration. The bullet had hit my rucksack and ended its flight in my can of beans and wieners.

Feeding belts of ammo into the M-60, I glanced quickly behind me to make sure we were covered and my heart stopped. A large, tall, strong, tobacco-chewing soldier lay frozen on the ground, unable to pull the trigger of his M-16, even to save his own life. His fear hit home with me. I looked over to our squad leader, lying on his stomach, emptying eighteen round clips of ammunition on full automatic from the M-16. For a split second, he stopped still, turned to look up at me and screamed, "Fuck, am I scared!" and just as quickly went back to emptying his clips of ammo. It was insanity unleashed. But in a weird way the battle sucked out and used all the pent up fear and tension in us.

The battle lasted into the darkness. When soldiers in helicopters knocked wooden boxes of ammo out to re-supply us, the boxes dropped through the trees, burst apart on impact and magazines of ammo flew everywhere. Little we cared, they were delivered and we needed them. It renewed our spirits to see them and the helicopters. Seeing them gave us the feeling of being connected, to know we were not alone.

My gunner was firing the M-60 at such a rapid pace that the barrel got too hot and began firing erratically. We changed it and he rattled on. The two of us were under cover behind a dead tree trunk lying on the ground. As I knelt next to him, feeding belts into the gun, the most bizarre thing happened. In an instant, a Vietcong raced across in front of us, firing his machine gun. The rounds ripped through that dead log, first on the far side of the gunner, then in between us, and then behind me but neither of us was hit. Each bullet came through that log exposing the fresh clean meat of its inside. For an instant I remember thinking how much like a movie it looked, but immediately the feverish fear of reality returned.

Fighting stopped in the darkness. What had been the energy of battle was now replaced with the trembling of nerves. I was drenched in sweat that was pouring off my shaking hands, soaking the cigarette I was trying to light, but I needed a smoke. Lit and soaked, only a few inhales were needed to smoke it to the butt. I was scared; every nerve in my body was on edge. Was it over? Would they come back? We slept very lightly that night.

During the next morning's jungle haze, my assignment was

to go out with another soldier and count the dead bodies. We neared a corpse, face down, on the jungle floor and the soldier with me tried to turn the body over with his foot. But the body had been so badly shot up that the soldier's foot only sank into the chest as if it were mush. There were massive blood trails from others who crawled or were dragged away. This was not the blood of a surface wound but the cavernous, dark, thick blood from massive intestinal wounds. My heart felt sick with the sight of the dead and wounded. I knew it could be my body someday. What was this war? Just sickness pretending to have a higher purpose. I remember turning from that mutilated corpse and walking back to our position when a bizarre happening occurred. Something left me. Something structural. My arms and shoulders drooped, my head sank, and my spine curled forward. What had left, though not physical, had seemed to support my physical bearing. I would later realize that it was my soul, my spirituality that had shattered and left me. By the time I went home, my soul would be empty, barren, and seemingly destroyed. Nothing would make sense anymore. Only the accumulation of negativity, evil, and hatred was left to haunt the vacant place and make its darkness blacker and blacker.

GOD REALLY DOES THIS?

CHAPTER TWO

I remember rolling up dead bodies in our rain ponchos. We tied them to long sticks and carried them out of the jungle as dead animals are carried on safaris. I could not believe the nice guy I had been raised to be was carrying dead human beings tied to poles - human beings we had killed. The Army only wanted enemy body count, numbers. There was no objective to this war as there had been in WWII. We did not have a maniac to stop, and I never heard it said that we had any goal to achieve. We were there because the people in the U.S. Government could not find the courage to stand up and say, "This war is wrong, we must stop it now!" I wished those people could have been there in combat, that they could be the ones carrying those dead bodies. How could they let us go on killing and being killed for no reason, while they argued over a useless war or the shape of a table at the Paris Peace Conferences?

We took the dead bodies to a nearby village that was thought to be supportive of the Viet Cong, and dumped them onto the dirt to check the villagers' reactions. Sadly enough, one woman ran to a corpse, crying: It was the body of her husband. She was arrested and taken away. We were never informed as to what happened to her or the other sympathizers. We didn't really want to know.

Another day my platoon was walking through tall elephant grass, under the usual tremendous stress and anxiety. Startled, by movement and Vietnamese voices a few feet to our right we frantically opened up machine gun fire. We had gunned down an old man and his son. Barefoot, dressed in rags, carrying only an old rusty machete, the two peasants had been searching for firewood to cook their food and make charcoal to sell. The old man probably could have cared less if his government was communist or not. He was just trying to keep his family fed and alive. They were in a woodcutters' zone - an insane idea to make some indistinguishable place on the map a neutral zone from combat. I stood over the old man's body lying in the grass, stared at his dead, wrinkled face with a white Ho Chi Minh beard, and a deep scream raged inside me: "What the fuck are we doing?" I thought how pathetic and repulsive this war was. No rational mind would ever put God's name on this insanity. More of my soul left that moment, and my posture sank further. We left the bodies where they had fallen. I wondered what their family members would feel when they discovered the loss. The cold, steel shield I was developing in my mind grew larger to keep me out of shock. Otherwise, I could not have gone on, and going on was the only choice.

When the Australian Army surprised an estimated five thousand North Vietnamese Regular Forces lodged in a huge and well-fortified jungle bunker complex, we were told (after listening to the raging sounds of that battle for two days) that the NVA were retreating under cover of night. We were assembled in small units and were carried by helicopter into the jungle to set up an ensnarement. After arranging a huge arc of ambushes, we were positioned in the NVA's supposed path of retreat. There was no way we had enough ammunition. If every bullet we fired killed one of them, we would still be overrun and annihilated. A retreating Army would be desperate and not allow a dozen guys to stop them. We were there only to identify the NVA position so heavy guns and air strikes could be brought in to obliterate them. Before help could get to us, we'd be overrun and dead. We were "expendable," the "price to be paid." I have never had such a sinking and despairing feeling as I did at that moment. Other human beings had no right to offer our lives for their meaningless goals! How could our lives be that useless and unimportant? I was at once emptied of shock and filled with fury. I wanted to get to those who were sending us to do this and drag their asses out where we were. I wanted to make them suffer and endure the same fear, humiliation, and degradation of life that they were dealing out. But there was no escape, nowhere to run: Our only choice was to face death. We prepared to die for a war we knew had no purpose, no legitimate goal; we knew our country was in no danger. However, the NVA, being knowledgeable jungle soldiers, evidently sent out a scout who spotted our ambushes, and so they avoided us and disappeared into the jungle. We never saw them.

Another time I came close to tasting death was when, but for the shout to "Stop!" from a Cambodian scout, the next step would have tripped the wire across the opening to an underground bunker, exploding a booby trap 2 feet from our faces, blowing us into the hereafter in unrecognizable pieces. The majority of time in the jungle, we were hyper vigilant yet monotonously trudging up and down the central highland mountains. We were constantly searching, our mental strings taut to the snapping point, looking for anything that moved, any sound or smell, booby traps, those damned trip wires, and that most frightening ordeal, "The Ambush." But what about those trip wires we would not be lucky enough to see? That was the ceaseless stress, hoping to spot the opponents and their traps before death grabbed us. That never-ending tension and anxiety caused long-lasting damage to my nervous system.

One hazy morning, we heard over our field radio that another of our battalion companies operating near us was engaged in a firefight with the Vietcong. The voice announced that one of the Vietcong soldiers killed was a woman, and that an American soldier, deciding he needed a souvenir, had cut off her breasts. Again I felt that unexplainable disgust in the human race, and another part of my soul seemed to leave. More and more the mental shield had to reinforce my backbone and pad my worn out mind.

On Easter Sunday, a Catholic chaplain came out to the jungle by helicopter to say Mass. Dressed in his camouflaged fatigues, he looked like one of us although he had no weapons. It was the one and only time I have been to Mass armed with a machine gun and hand grenades. Before beginning his service, the chaplain placed his white vestment over his head, and the brilliant whiteness against the dark green jungle background gave him the appearance of an apparition right out of the Bible. During the sermon he said that two Americans from another battalion had been killed the day before. "And now," the Chaplain told us, "I want you to go out and get two of the enemy!" His words stunned me and left me bitter. He could have said, "Let us pray for their souls," or "I'm going with you to get two of them," or "I hope this tragedy of war ends soon and we can all go home." I stared at him in disbelief, wanting to stuff my M-16 in his hands and scream, "If you want two of them killed, go do it yourself, asshole!"

What was this guy doing in the military anyway? When did Catholicism - whose very laws, the ten commandments, excommunicate offenders and condemn them to eternal suffering in hell - give in and ally itself with an organization whose primary purpose was to kill? When did the Church decide it was acceptable to wear the uniform, rank, medals, eat the food and form a brotherhood with an organization that purely trampled on those sacred beliefs that are its identity and power in guiding the souls and spirits of its followers to heaven? But I had yet to reach my twenty-first birthday and although the outlook for doing so was in question by the moment, I had not lived long enough to accumulate sufficient wisdom and knowledge to understand.

Thirty years later, I still have not gained a sufficient quantity of either to change my opinion. The jungle Mass experience profoundly tested my belief in God. Thoughts no longer came casually to my mind; they came screaming at me in a rage of disbelief in the human race. How could God allow this thing called war? If He was all-powerful, why did He let these horrible things happen and why didn't He soothe my soul? Was there really a God? It no longer felt like it.

After all of these experiences and various others, my soul felt totally exhausted, and the mental barrier I had developed to protect myself was just about all that was left. The empty look (the "1000-yard stare") was all I held in my eyes. I cannot explain the disgust, hatred, and lack of trust I developed for the U.S. Government, the military, and human beings. It remains my hope that time absolves the soldiers, and properly blames the Federal Government. We might have been as great as any generation of fighting soldiers had we been given a legitimate reason to defend home and family.

DESTRUCTION OF A SOUL

CHAPTER THREE

They say all is fair in love and war – anything goes. I don't know about love but that is definitely true in combat. When I returned from Vietnam one truth was inescapable – my sense of isolation from everyone. The old values, goals and desires no longer existed for me. I felt an undeniable separation from society. I thought people could never comprehend my experiences in war, and I no longer accepted society's values.

My inability to find a way to explain the experience of war created a barrier between society and myself. I could not understand why humans did the things they did to each other in the name of war. My time in Vietnam had been highly traumatic. The technology designed for warfare and killing was not in my vocabulary, so I tried to put my experiences safely out of reach in my mind, behind the protective barrier. It would have been unsafe for me to lower the barrier and face that knowledge inside, much less try and explain the pure absurdity of war to others. I could tell war stories, but could not begin to explain why human beings engage in war. I could only recount these stories when I worked from behind my "facade." I still can't truly touch what happened without dissolving in tears.

Some experiences must be buried away, and have no value

when told. Over time I realized it was OK not to be able to fully explain war. After all, we went to war to protect those at home from knowing the insanity of warfare. If they do not fully understand, oddly enough, that is part of the goal. I would never wish those at home to experience such atrocities.

I have five wonderful sisters who are all good and loving mothers. I have been with one or the other, or with several at one time when, with their young children, we have been to the grocery store, the mall, the airport, or county fair. I have always been amazed at their vigilance, that second nature they possess to be aware of their children's whereabouts every second. They are never long distracted before shooting a glance to be assured of the children's safety. "You stay near me; stay where I am; stay here in front of me," they murmur. They are always aware that a real danger exists in the world around them. The fear of a child being kidnapped is punishing enough. I have witnessed the flash of panic come into their eyes, and have watched them drop everything and dash madly in search of a lost child only to find him or her casually poking around their new surroundings. The relief for the mother is an exclamation of thankfulness sometimes spiced with a little anger.

But imagine when it does not end that way. Imagine the mother who, in her frantic desperation, does not find the child, and must face the reality that her child actually has been kidnapped. Gone! How horrible the devastation to mind and soul, the anger and hatred of the kidnapper and herself: "Who could do such a thing?" "Why would anyone do this?" "This can't be happening to me!"

Think of the sleepless nights, the nightmares, and the loss of life's familiar joys and importance. Work would mean nothing, money would mean nothing, material things the same. Old beliefs are shattered, reality is now of a cruel and insane world. The parent's guilt is overwhelming. Although she continues to be a mother, it will never be the same as for mothers who still have their children. No day will ever pass again without thoughts of her child. The anguish and emptiness will turn to anger and hatred. She will see other mothers with their children and she will never know the happiness of watching children grow. She will never know the joys of her own life, and she will never, ever, be able to completely explain the nightmare of her loss. No one will ever completely understand except by experiencing the same fate.

So it is with a soldier who has suffered combat trauma. He is still a man, an American, but his view of reality has changed. There was no way I could have explained the difference I felt inside as I was on my way home from Vietnam. As the Boeing 707 taxied down the runway at Bien Hoa Airfield, the soldiers inside erupted into screams of joy, hoots and hollers, and fraternal handshakes. As the plane took off, a quick silence replaced the noise, faces pressed to the windows. I stared at the cratered landscape below. To see the country from the air gave me the last wrenching view of the savagery that humans had inflicted on each other. How could people live there? How could they find any sanctuary in that blistered, gutted, and destroyed terrain? Another round of well wishing and hollers sounded as the plane settled into flight and then all was quiet again, faces pressed back to the windows. We flew out over the beautiful water of the South China Sea. I remember just staring transfixed at the coast of South Vietnam as it slowly disappeared behind us. I remember so clearly having the most bizarre sense that I was flying out of some horrifying, clouded, nightmarish memory. For a moment I was not really sure it had even happened. It had to be a dream; it was too insane to have been real. More screams of joy followed, hugs and handshakes, and then the bottles of booze came out. "IT" (War) was over! Or so we thought. The plane was filled with drunken celebration. I got completely drunk and passed out twice before we landed in Honolulu. I was spiritually, mentally, and physically exhausted.

Two thoughts had given me hope, and a place to go in my mind to escape the drudgery of war. One was the constant thought of being with my high school sweetheart, whom I truly loved and had married while on leave. Many said it was a match made in heaven, and it very well might have been if man had not made war on earth. She was nineteen and I was twenty when I went off to war. We had both been so afraid; the possibility of not seeing each other again was enough to break my heart. We had dreams, big dreams: professions, children, beautiful home and life together. I can't tell you how many times the thought of our future gave me the courage to go on. While in the jungle, over and over I would hear American Forces Radio play a song we had shared I fought back tears and wanted only to go home to her. I especially remember Elton John's, "This is Your Song." Missing her became physical pain and anguish.

And how could I forget the excitement and anticipation of mail call? This is the most important and joyful time at war, especially letters from loved ones, scented letters, words that connected you to home life and sanity. It was on one such mail call that we were huddled around reading letters, some quietly to themselves, others out loud, sharing happy messages that distracted us from our stressful situation. Our squad leader, deeply tanned, days without a shower, fatigued from war, and covered in red dust, sat on sand bags reading a letter from home. His hands suddenly dropped to his knees; he stared straight ahead, and his face went blank and pale as if his very spirit was leaving him. When pushed to explain what was wrong, he answered in a mechanical voice, "My wife has met another man and wants a divorce."

I was crushed for him; no weapon of any destructive force could have delivered a more deadly strike. It was obvious he no longer cared about life or death. At home he would have had access to therapy, antidepressants, and sleep aids. There in the jungle he simply suffered. The raging insanity that had come to haunt me had put this woman on a list of people who deserved a bullet more than those we were firing at here. I thank the Good Lord I never suffered this man's emotional damage.

But now, I had made it and was going home to the touch of my wife's soft skin, the kiss of her lips, her beautiful soft hair, the fragrance of her perfume, the sound of her voice, her singing and laughter. I couldn't wait to hold her hand and lay by her side. I'd been in the Army less than two years, I'd been to war, and we had yet to have a normal chance outside the panic and fear of losing each other to make love. I would have run home from Hawaii if I thought I could have gotten there faster than on military transport.

The other thought that occupied my dreams was the G.I. Bill for college. Coming from a family of ten kids and divorced parents, college would have been a long shot without the G.I. Bill. I was going to use this opportunity and fulfill my dream of becoming a college graduate. I dreamed of the different fields I could study, campus life, football Saturdays with marching bands, stadiums filled with colors, laughter, cheers and groans, and just the fun of a fabulous life. I thought of all the careers I might choose: an engineer, or a lawyer, or maybe a scientist. It was a joy just to think about the possibilities.

Flying into San Francisco from Hawaii, we landed at Travis Air Force Base only about eighteen hours out of the combat zone. I had flown out of the same base one year earlier going to Vietnam. I remembered that time now, how scared we were and how long twelve months as combat infantrymen seemed. Twelve thousand years would have seemed the same. When we had left Travis Air Force Base going to Vietnam, we were told of a great steak dinner that awaited every soldier on his return. I remember thinking of the impossibility of surviving long enough to return for that dinner. It seemed horrifyingly impossible, and that steak dinner seemed a foolish dream. It would probably never be mine to enjoy. Twelve months was just too long to survive at those odds. But here I was back at Travis Air Force Base! ALIVE! Not in a box! The steak dinner that seemed an impossibility one year ago, the futility of a thought that I could survive to enjoy it, now meant nothing. There was a huge price to be paid for beating the odds and living, and that price was paid with my soul. I know a steak dinner can satisfy the pangs of the stomach, but I had never heard that a steak dinner could repair a damaged soul. All around me, I could hear my own thoughts put to words by other soldiers on the plane: "I just want to go home, and I'll buy my own goddamned steak dinner!" "What we've seen and done, for a lousy steak dinner? Thanks, but kiss my ass!" That steak dinner, which had represented survival, now had no meaning at all. It disgusted me.

I've often heard that the eyes are the windows to the soul. I brought back few photos of Vietnam, but I have two that I treasure. One is of me when I first arrived, the other several days before I left to come home. The first photo shows eyes that were alive with expression, set in a tan, healthy face and a body well fed: The bright eyes of a typically healthy twenty-year-old American middle class man. The second photo has little resemblance to the first. They are not of the same human being. War, its traumas, the minute-to-minute vigilance needed to stay alive, the stress to not be responsible for another American's death, had reduced my weight by over thirty pounds. In the second photo, my face is gaunt and grey, with a vacant expression, my cheeks sunken in. But my eyes are what are so noticeably different; my eyes are green, but not in this photo. They are black and empty, sunken into the dark shadows that surround them; so empty one can see the void where my soul had been.

I live in Wisconsin where ice fishing is popular. With an auger, a 10-inch fishing hole is bored in the solid ice of a lake. Envision a natural, annual fall event in these lakes: The warmer, surface waters exchange places with the colder, deeper waters, and the lake life follows the warmer waters to the lake bottom, leaving the surface waters freezing and empty of life. If one stands on the ice looking down into one of these holes, one can feel the cold, lifeless depth below. It is the same as my eyes in the second photo, empty of life, cold and hollow, with frozen ice around the hole. I had the sense that something very dear was leaving me when I saw that first dead Vietcong. Combat after combat had stolen more of my soul, until it now showed up as the darkness of every evil emotion. Nineteen years of middle class American life as a Catholic, and the teachings that life gave out all failed in warfare. Only anger, fear, hatred, guilt and shame remained. So many years ago I had been taught the following lessons: "Turn the other cheek"; "Thou shalt not kill"; "It is a sin to tell a lie"; "Thou shalt not covet"; "Be kind to others"; and "Be compassionate to the less fortunate and help them." All of these I had to unlearn as I endured combat.

Everything spiritual that had formed the foundations of my soul felt like a lie. My soul had been scooped and cleaned out, just as one scrapes a pumpkin to make a jack-o-lantern. Every seed, every strand of pulp of my beliefs was gone. I was souled out, and the windows to my soul were positive proof.

RAGE BECOMES ME

CHAPTER FOUR

So, I passed up the steak dinner. I despised the Army for the great disappointment it had become to me; the honor of history was nowhere to be found in the great lie of that war. I despised what was allowed to happen to U.S. soldiers and their families and the Vietnamese people, in cowardly defense of that lie. I have never wanted to be so far away from anything in my life as I did the Army, the government, and the American people. In Hawaii, I went directly to the building where I would be issued my state side dress uniform, travel pay, reassignment orders, and a plane ticket home to Wisconsin. After tailors took my measurements for coat, pants, shirt, and hat size, I waited for my uniform to be altered. At that point I would have gone home in my underwear. But I abided by the rules, waited for the uniform (whose destiny for incineration was only days away), in a huge sitting area with other soldiers. While there, an officer announced that anyone who wanted to sign out of the Army permanently could do so. Those who had not served in the Army eighteen months (the time required to be eligible for benefits) could sign out permanently if they signed away the G.I. Bill. Again the Army and government embittered me. We had been to WAR. Why couldn't they wave the time limit in appreciation? Word on the street was that too many infantry soldiers were coming home and the Army had nothing for them to do. I had gone to basic training, advanced infantry training, had a thirty-day leave and a year at war - a total of about seventeen and one-half months of active service - but they were not going to forego the half-month. In no way was I going to sign away what I had dreamed of for so long: college. I took my uniform, assembled the medals, ropes and insignias on it, took my ticket and reassignment orders, and raced to the airport to catch a flight for thirty days of leave. This leave and a few more months of active service seemed a piece of joyous, glorious cake, and then I would go to college.

Other than my stint in the military, the furthest I had been from home was the one time I'd traveled the 90 miles from Milwaukee to the Illinois border with my dad to buy margarine, during the days the Dairy State of Wisconsin would allow only the much more expensive butter to be sold. The military I became part of had no officer higher than rank of Captain in combat with us in the jungle. That military attempted to inspire us to greatness by offering a three-day "in-country R & R" to every soldier for each Viet Cong or NVA he killed. This was not honor, nor glory. To me it was bounty hunting.

Over time, the two most frequent questions I've been asked as a Vet are: "Did you have to kill people?" and "Did you see hand-to-hand combat?" The first question displays a protected society's lack of comprehension that the war was real, and that they might be face-to-face with someone who has killed another human being. Also, I often consider the possibility that embedded in their curiosity is the question of their capability to kill. It is part of the disconnection between the protected and those who have had to deal with the reality, and is further proof to me that society can't explain or fully understand war. A soldier's job is to protect society from that very reality and understanding.

However, I can always answer the second more easily: Did I see hand-to-hand combat? "Yes!" (And I always have to laugh.)

"Once in an airport in San Francisco, and once in Chicago!" Nevertheless, the background of my true experiences in combat explain how the now war-experienced soldier tries to readjust to a changed home, and comes to realize how fundamentally he himself has changed.

Arriving home, the shock of reentry was immediate. I was different, something was not right; everything was not right! I was edgy and couldn't sit still. The dreams of the perfect green lawns, the picture book house, the loving perfect families and society, melted quickly, like light falling snow. Life at home was not a glorious dream, instead it was real, and had routines and problems. It was not the Garden of Eden I had envisioned while in the hell of Vietnam. The emotional wall I had developed to protect me from the shocks of war and the devastation to my soul, which I thought would dissolve now that I was home, did not disappear, but only became more evident. I was no longer with other soldiers who had also developed that shield and shared the experiences of war. I was with those who couldn't understand. I felt totally isolated.

During that thirty-day leave I could not stand to be in crowds. I was unable to feel comfortable in conversation, be around loud noise or fast activity. I slowly separated myself from people, places, activities, and life. Nothing gave me pleasure. Simple, joys, goals, dreams of new cars, money, stereos, job choices and advancements, the fun of going to movies, pro sporting games, and picnics found no response in me. Everyday life seemed to mean nothing. But why? What was wrong? I was constantly haunted by anxiety, restlessness, nightmares, and a sense that I just could not understand, much less organize or calm. The unreal experiences of war plagued my mind. This confusion and inability to understand myself added additional fear to that already buried behind the barrier protecting my psyche. I felt that the failure of my belief system left me with no comprehension of who I was. There is probably no more dreadful fear than that of losing your mind. Nor is there a greater struggle than to keep that torment hidden. Years later I would find I had no choice, those festering emotions were coming out, like it or not. I would have to face them, or take the "final solution" for the pains that haunted my mind.

The relationship with my wife that sustained me during war was in trouble immediately on my return. The perfect marriage made in heaven, the perfect meshing of two lovers and friends was unraveling quickly and very painfully for both of us. We were just two young adults unprepared for that destructive, incomprehensible set of events in our lives. It had been too much to absorb for both of us. While I was away, my wife had been alone at home. She had no family, no friends, neighbors, or anyone who had a husband or boyfriend at war; she was alone in her experience. I was the one off to war, and knew exactly where I was and what danger I was in, or not in. She had only a fearful imagination. All the horrible scenarios the human mind can dream up terrorized her. The worst was to picture that day when someone would come to the door to announce the death of her love. In the perfect world of retrospection, I wish I had not been awash in my own anxiety and pain. I wish I had spent at least some effort on understanding her heartbreaking experience. I didn't. I couldn't. I was barely hanging on in the battle to save my own mind, and could not realize how devastating my time at war had been for her.

Several weeks after my return, I noticed that my wife was angered at the attention I received as a veteran. She told me she felt she deserved consideration as much or more than I did, because the war had been more difficult and painful for her. I was shocked. It seemed impossible that she could be serious. I had been to war! How could she beat that pain and suffering? Years later she would call to tell me that she finally realized the war was harder on me than her. I don't know that I will ever understand how difficult situations like that are for the ones left behind. Had I the wisdom (whether I agreed or not), I might have at least heard the message that she had suffered deeply during that time of war, and needed compassion and understanding as much as I.

Again, we were young adults just beginning life. We had barely begun the adventure of getting to know each other. How could she have been expected to understand me, when I could not understand myself? It had to be heartbreaking for her to experience the breaking of such a deep bond. We just didn't have the answers. One remedy we did incorporate would prove to be a sad addition to the misery. We both used alcohol in great quantities simply to numb the emotional agony we were feeling. We just could not help each other.

The two of us left for Texas and Fort Hood, and I was happy to have my wife with me. The thought of life alone again in the Army was as unpleasant a thought as jumping into the pit of any outhouse. We took a small, dilapidated apartment off base. We expected to be there about five months, then my two-year obligation to the Army would end and I would begin working towards my college degree. Strange things kept happening in the service that contradicted my impression of an American Army. It happened in Vietnam, and it happened at Fort Hood. Could all military administrations before us have had such problems with drugs and alcohol? Had racism always been as open and hostile on all sides? Were lower echelon troops so distrusting and hateful of higher-ranking officers? Was all this disruption apparent in the two World Wars and the Korean War? I didn't know, but these problems were strongly present during my time in Vietnam and at Fort Hood. Later on, while interviewing WWII veterans and wives of WWII veterans, the answers to some of my questions would become apparent.

The company I was assigned to at Fort Hood was made up of infantry soldiers who had just returned from war. We all had similar traits of bitterness, anger, hatred and rebellion against the war, disappointment and distrust for the Army and the government. The mental shields we had developed were still in place, even though we were now half a world away from the war.

It would take years for me, to dismantle this cold, hard shield. For some it would never lower and would cheat its bearer out of years of inner peace. For many it would be the end of life, a shield too painful to live with.

It was our mandatory military duty to report each day for morning formation and roll call. Assembled as a company unit, we were to be properly dressed in complete military uniform and lined up in platoon ranks. We needed to be identified as "present" when called by name, and then given our daily assignments or duties. KP and other menial tasks were the only duties they could find for us. After all, a war hardened infantry division in the middle of Texas was of little use. Skills enabling us to lob grenades or machine gun folks down were of little use in the middle of Texas.

We were an unnecessary burden on the military, just mouths to feed. We were hardened, embittered veterans; many had lost all respect for most officers above captain's rank and did not see them as brave military leaders. The disgust and hatred of the war and the U.S. government left many unable and unwilling to participate in the rituals of their game. When called to formation, guys showed up with shirts unbuttoned, no hat, pants not tucked into boots, and cigarettes dangling in their mouths. I have to admit it was one of the few times military life brought a smile to my face. At the call to "ATTENTION!" most guys didn't move a muscle, but stood any way but at attention. Most were defiant and simply had had enough. Platoon sergeants would yell and scream threats of all sorts of punishment, which didn't cause a flinch of fear in any face nor shift the posture of anyone. The sergeant would have gotten more response from a granite outcrop. In its own bizarre way, it was hilarious. Frustrated, the sergeant would go on to call names and give out daily duty assignments, all of which were quickly disobeyed as everyone left for town.

Before we were dismissed we had to go on police call, a military name given to the lining up of the troops in a straight line across one end of the company grounds. On command, the line of men would walk across the grounds and police the area or pick up papers, garbage, and cigarette butts. That would have been "textbook." We were anything but textbook. While reaping more fury and threats of dishonorable discharges, our line would walk across the company grounds, but not one body bent over to pick up anything. It was just a casual stroll with guys talking, carrying on, smoking cigarettes, and adding to the litter on the ground. We were uncontrollable, unaffected by threats and not about to be reduced to garbage pickers. What could they do? Court martial a company of Vietnam Veterans who had just returned from service to their country for not picking up cigarette butts? This was the first time I heard a veteran respond to a threat with a line that would become popular: "What are you gonna do, send me to Vietnam?" It made me laugh and that felt good, unusual but good.

This confrontational circus lasted about two weeks. We were then told there were too many idle infantry forces. Anyone who wanted out of the Army could sign out. To this day it is one of the greatest gifts I have ever received. I had now been in the service just over eighteen months and qualified for the G.I. Bill. Few messages ever brought such relief and happiness. I put in for an immediate discharge. All that was left, as it is said, was to "muster out." This included signing out of the different Army sections: headquarters, turning in all military equipment, receiving final travel pay, and to the medical station for a final physical. I had had severe headaches while on leave and the doctor at the VA center near my home had given me aspirin and codeine. I had no other bodily problems so the physical would be a breeze. The final step was a test that had become standard in the military, the urine test for drug abuse. I had never really been a drug user so that, too, would be a breeze. I finished all the stations and went back to my wife and the apartment in Killeen to wait for all that paper work to be processed. "A couple days," they had said. I was so anxious to get out of there that I could not relax or sleep, and passed the time killing the herds of flies that came through what supposedly represented screens on our apartment windows.

WHERE DID THE HONOR GO?

CHAPTER FIVE

The day before I was to get out of the Army forever, two MPs pulled up in front of our apartment. Armed with 45 caliber pistols, they came to the front door and announced, "We have a warrant for your arrest." I was dumbfounded. The shock was stunning. I hadn't even jaywalked, what could it possibly be? The MPs had no idea what the warrant was for; only orders to bring me back to base. As they put me into the jeep, I was empty of all emotion but rage. I was taken to a building and escorted into an office where a wretchedly arrogant Major, who was a psychiatrist, was sitting behind a desk. Rudely and without introduction he stated, "Where did you get the morphine? Your urine test came back positive for morphine." I could hardly think I was so shaken. My mind was racing! Morphine, where would I get morphine in Texas? I wasn't even a pot smoker! This was ludicrous, insane. It must be a mistake; had to be. "Are you taking any medication?" he asked.

"Just aspirin and codeine for headaches," I responded. He informed me that those could not leave an indication of morphine in a drug test. He said it so quickly, without giving it any thought, I could tell by the look on his face and his manner that he could care less what I said. Convinced of the lab results, he had no desire to think otherwise. He went on to inform me that I would be put in detox for a month. After that, I would be sent to drug rehabilitation for one year in the hospital at Fort Hood, and finally, five years of outpatient rehabilitation at a hospital nearest my home. I felt like I had been run over by a tank. I could think of nothing other than I could take no more goddamned military. I could not mentally make it through one more day of oppressive military life, much less months and years. An armed guard took me to an abandoned WWII barracks on an isolated area of the base. I was searched for drugs, my clothes were taken away, and I was issued the proper uniform for that place. I was allowed a few personal things that were, of course, inspected for hidden contraband. About twenty other drug addicts were already assigned their new multi-year contracts. Assigned an Army cot and footlocker in a large open barracks, I walked slowly to my bunk in disbelief.

I had grown up during the sixties: drugs, free sex, the great hippie movement, head shops, and all the other customs of the era. But drug addicts, the hardcore users who think drugs are everything and are willing to do anything it takes to secure drugs, are pathetic. And drug dealers have always been the waste from the sewer of the human race! Hell, I had changed the group of friends I hung out with in high school because they preferred drugs and I preferred beer. It was not a pious judgment; drug use just had no attraction for me.

So now there I was in a damn drug ward with a disgusting bunch of scum who had achieved every requirement needed to be there. I stood at the end of my bunk, still in shock. I looked around the hall at my new platoon. My eyes stopped on each guy's face. What a sad assembly of human beings! They all appeared the same: colored headbands, peace signs on chains around their necks, peace sign patches sewn to shirtsleeves, and most in the glassy eyed semi-comatose drug state. Few were moving around, most just lying on their bunks. When they did move, it was in slow motion; when they spoke, the voices were slow and slurred. When a head turned, the eyes were late in catching up with it. Eyes were half closed for some, closed for others. These guys were off somewhere else, drifting who knew or cared where. When one did come around long enough to notice my recent arrival (the new guy!), an arm would raise slowly, eyes glassy and half shut, the fingers would slowly form the V of a peace sign and a voice inside the carcass would slur out "Whaaats happpeninnng, man?" I wondered if the question was about what was happening with me or with them.

At the end of the barracks a medical technician of some sort, dressed in white, sat behind a desk. He was the barrack's monitor watching over the pride of the Army. After taking all of this in, I finally realized that a radio was blaring acid rock music and I was glad to be taking aspirin and codeine; that music gave me headaches and tortured my ears. So many thoughts went through my head at such a rate that I could hardly grab onto one long enough to make any sense out it. I do remember sitting on my bunk, not just thinking, but also knowing that, again, I would not last. This place had nothing to redeem itself; there were no books, no magazines, no TV, no puzzles, no exercise, no time outside the barracks, nothing. I was doomed to pass the time with semi-comatose drug addicts blaring acid rock music with nowhere to escape. I knew it would not be long before that barracks turned violent. I was concerned that the stored anger and bitterness of war, the loss of so many decent men who just wanted to go home to wives, children, girlfriends and families, would explode. I had been in that barracks less than half an hour when I gritted my teeth to keep from slamming that radio against a wall or throwing it out the window. What would I do the next day or next week?

At times like this I would remember the experiences of war. Like when we were on a forward base waiting for helicopters to pick us up for a mission, shooting the bull and exchanging stories. A guy from another platoon pulled out a picture of his beautiful blonde twin daughters. He bragged as a loving father brags, told how much he loved them. The picture made his eyes sparkle. The next day he was killed, dead, gone. I know this may sound cruel and judgmental, but in the anger of that time in the drug ward, I wished that father, who was honorable, and others like him who had been killed, could trade places and go home to their families and these guys, wasting their lives on drugs, could take their places in those graves. Their lives appeared to mean little to them, anyway.

There is a sad but true residue of war for me. Having participated in the killing of people I did not know nor have reason to kill, at times I have a thought that just comes out of that dark side without being asked. There are people at home that I had a more rational reason to kill. While in that drug ward this thought came up again and again. " I could just shoot your fuckin' ass!" This thought has surfaced many times over the years and is always confronted by the civilized part of me. I am not proud of this thought but understand its connection to my instinctive, animal survival that was pulled from the depth of me at war. I am human and accept that.

My first day in detox I was allowed one phone call home, but what would I tell my wife? How this would crush her! I had no choice but to tell her. She was devastated! She knew I never took drugs and also believed there must have been a mistake, mislabeled urine sample, something. I asked for and was given a second phone call to my father-in-law, a doctor. I told him about the morphine results and the aspirin and codeine. The first thing he said was, "That stupid ass, of course they would turn up the same, the damn things come from the same plant!" I was so furious with that psychiatrist my rage was uncontrollable. I paced and paced, burning off the fury. It was late Friday afternoon and the psychiatrist would not be back until Monday. Had he still been there, without a doubt, I would have stormed his office and laid him out cold. Not only because he was wrong but also because he had been too damn lazy to pick up a book and find out! It was easier for him just to pass off what he didn't know at the expense of years of my life. I guess he was about as excited with military life as I, and just wanted to finish his tour of duty and get out; all of his professionalism to be saved for happier civilian life and not wasted on the military. I would hold that anger against that arrogant man for years, and dreamed of getting my hands on his throat! The weekend would pass punishing minute by punishing minute, but I had a spark of hope for Monday, to convince the psychiatrist to research his decision.

I quickly learned the system in detox. We were isolated intentionally; this way, when the drugs wore off and there was no re-supply, an addict would go into withdrawal. The medic at the desk appeared disgusted, bored, and wanting to be somewhere else. He showed no interest in communicating, counseling or getting to know anyone. In fact, he was there for one reason: When someone did go into withdrawal, his job was to make sure that person was taken by ambulance for medical help. But withdrawal was more than that. It was the final proof, the evidence, above all lies of denial, that one was on drugs.

Though well intentioned, the detox program was wildly erroneous and tragic. Strange, because, though isolated, we did have to eat. Three meals a day were brought from the main base. KP (kitchen police) was typically the lowest duty the Army offered and often given as a punishment, and this included serving food. So take a wild guess! Who do you think brought our three meals a day? Officers? NCOs? Nope. Low echelon troublemakers serving their punishment on KP. And besides food, guess what else they could provide! That's right! DRUGS! The pots of food were brought in and set out on a long table. As we walked in single file to be served our food, on passing the last food server, there on the table, the last station, was an array of drugs neatly laid out as jewelry on display, every color and size. I hadn't known that people with that habit used so many drugs. And guess what else! If they didn't have what you wanted, you could place an order for it! The servers happily and professionally took your order and would bring what you wanted at a later meal. It was tragic that these guys would not get the help they needed. Who knew which guys would die or overdose from the next KP serving? It must have driven the project directors crazy trying to figure out why these guys, who they knew were drug addicts, were not going into withdrawal. Drug addicts are the sneakiest con artists I have ever met.

Over the weekend more guys arrived in the detox center, including others who did not appear to be drug addicts. One tall, lanky, young guy from Tennessee -a really nice, back woodsy, minister type - came in, his head, legs and arms bandaged. He had been in a car accident on the base, was sent to the base hospital, and was given barbiturates for the pain at the hospital, then flunked the urine test for barbiturates at the same hospital, and was assigned to the drug rehab program. A gentler man had never reached such heights of anger; he beat me on this scale. We quickly became companions, mostly from necessity, but I generally enjoyed his conversation and calm manner. There were other similar cases including high-ranking officers who were flunking the drug test for heart medication and the like. They, of course, were kept at the hospital, not with us.

Monday morning I was reevaluated and released. But the bitter anger would last for years, and the anxiety had caused deep strain for me. There is a dream I remember having several times when I was young. I was being chased by a monster and couldn't get away. My legs were so heavy I couldn't move them, and my feet seemed stuck in oozing clay. The monster would always get just close enough to grab me when I would be startled into the most heart pounding, sweaty, wakefulness. The Army paralleled that nightmare. I never tried to decipher the monster dream, but awakening from the nightmare of the Army and war was not easy. I would spend years trying to understand it. Monday when I woke from the drug ward nightmare, I had no idea that a new emotional war was building inside me.

My wife and I left, or better, ran out of Texas. Arriving home, I immediately felt isolated again. Life around me seemed as irrational as a Salvador Dali painting, confusing, disjointed. Life no longer made sense to me as it had before war. I think the people around me had the same sense about me. My wife was unable to get through to me because I could not explain what my mind was thinking - it was too dark. The goals and dreams that had been such saviors during war were gone. I couldn't comprehend why people were so absorbed in material possessions: cars, stereos, clothes and ownership of this and that. They seemed to live just to own things, and to get jobs that would give them not joy but money. For me, these things made no sense and could do nothing to restore my damaged soul. I was not able to get back in the game of American life. I know that many different trauma victims get relief and compassionate understanding by being with someone that shares that trauma. I did have that opportunity in the VFW or American Legion, but for some reason was not drawn to them. I would come to understand why years later.

Soon after my return from Texas, I was in trouble mentally and knew it. The rumblings of another thought would replace one incomplete thought and that one replaced by yet another and another. My mind was on fast forward while constantly changing topics; totally short-circuiting. This was a fear unlike the fear of physical death at war. Was I insane or on my way? My body was also confounding me. In bed at night before sleep, the muscles in my arms would twitch uncontrollably, and during the day my teeth would chatter rapidly. Not grind, but chatter. Years of this chattering left my upper front teeth so worn and thin, the dentist would need to build them back up with an epoxy or cap them.

I desperately sought help at the local Veterans Hospital and was assigned to the outpatient care of a kind, older psychologist. I learned that she had raised a family before returning to study and become licensed in her field. She was near retirement as evidenced by the hearing aid, the volume of which she controlled to tune in or out depending on her interest in what I was saying. Sitting tensely in a chair next to her desk, I noticed that she looked at the papers on her desk, or ahead at the wall, and with an occasional startle, would perk up, put her hand up to the hearing aid, adjust the volume and say, "I'm sorry, what was that you just said?" Months of therapy convinced me she was in low volume, drifting off to plan her retirement and how that joyous time would be spent. Never did we talk about my war experiences; we focused mainly on my dissolving marriage.

After more than a year of friendly meetings with this woman, I only wanted to be kind to her, not upset nor push her to early retirement in her somewhat frail state. I retired from therapy without notice of significant improvement. This approach to PTSD would improve dramatically at the VA during 1980 and 1990, when I would again seek help.

My wife and I were two young, lost souls, wandering in a marriage that was overwhelmed by experiences we could not process. Traumas left a horrible seething wound. And worse, we could not walk together emotionally because the traumas were different for each of us. Our individual traumas needed attention, and we just could not understand each other's experience. The wedge was driven deeper. We would spend several punishing years together, both choosing alcohol to mask what we were not armed to handle or solve.

It was such a tragedy. We separated and then divorced. I was now alone with a frightening mind I could not face, and a soul gutted smooth to the walls of everything that had been spiritual. I was a shell hiding a mass of internal devastation and negative emotions. But I was a veteran: Society's conscience needed to believe that guys do go off to war, do that insane activity and do come home unaffected. Over the years, I cannot say how many, many times people have said to me in one way or another "I know a Vietnam Vet and man is he screwed up!" All the while not realizing they were speaking to one of us! This phrase has always represented how little, Americans know the reality of warfare, and how irresponsible historians are for their representation of it.

Most Americans are struck by fear at the sight of a fist fight; cannot look at blood; cannot stop at a car accident; are horrified to think some intruder might be in their home; petrified that someone may be following them, and are traumatized by a pet dying or being injured. When a police officer draws his weapon, fires one round wounding or killing a criminal, he or she is immediately taken off street duty and psychological counseling is offered. When a seventeen or eighteen-year-old high school student is killed in a car accident, grief counselors and psychologists are immediately dispatched to the school to help all students, even though these students may have not seen the accident or may not even know the victim. Within a year, some of these same students may be at war and expected to witness savagery far greater than a car accident; expected to see this savagery over prolonged periods of time without suffering psychological affects. A soldier must have in his or her soul a reason to kill; this is the true balancing factor to maintaining some sanity. But society must, out of absolute need to believe, think young men and women should come home from the brutal insanity of war as if they had been on a luxury cruise around the world. Society needs that security. To me, an even more frightening scenario would be the guy who does come home from war and is exactly the same guy he had been before. Who could experience war and not be screwed up? That would be a scary person. But that is who I tried to be: an unaffected person, and I designed and performed a masterful job of concealing the truth.

I constantly worked on the construction of my beautiful facade to show society. I have read that everyone uses some type of mask to disguise some inner unsettled emotions, the desire to please, or a sense of inadequacy, the pretense being used to enhance one's public appearance. The facade I was developing to hide my shattered insides would be a completely new me, a new personality. I had to do this just to exist, to get by, to show my family, friends, and society that I was the veteran who had done his duty at war and was not screwed up. This was what I came to feel society needed to see, to soothe away the guilt and feel safe. But society came to disillusion me by its negative reactions to and lack of regard for its own military. The heartless expressions of individuals and groups that demoralized their own Army and inspired the enemy Army were a staggering piece of reality for me at that point in my life. This left me alone and even more isolated. My sense of anger, dislocation, and a growing coldness in place of loyalty made me feel there was no place for me in America.

DESPERATE ISOLATION

CHAPTER SIX

I spent most of my time sitting quietly in bars, with a mind that would not stop making noise and gnawing at me. I never caused trouble, never really talked to anyone; just sat drinking until I'd had enough to go home and sleep. Maybe I hoped the alcohol would anesthetize me through the terrifying nightmares: Purely inconsiderate nightmares that didn't care if I was tired, and certainly didn't care if I awakened trembling and drenched in sweat. They were determined to have things their own way and wreak havoc with me as they chose. I learned that even if a person might care that he had a job to get to the next day and desperately needed rest and restoration, nightmares are only fueled to deeper torment by these facts. And nightmares will continue pleasing themselves with their twisted, irrational movies until they find they can cause no more mental destruction. Then they will sneak off to find another soul to haunt. Nightmares cannot be disciplined, punished, or even threatened; they are ultimate bullies that come when they please. Not even the alcohol could keep them in abeyance.

The next day would be the same routine. Having no way to explain what was going on in my mind, alcohol was where I ran to hide to try and forget. Today I jokingly tell the story of

43

the night I went out to a party and came home two years later. Those two years are not much to write about, because it was repetitive, monotonous drinking and refusal to acknowledge the shattered mind and soul. There were occasional affairs, the ones a lonely, lost person hiding in alcohol always finds. The kind involving a partner who is also lost, simply a void trying to fill another void. Relationships floated in the facade, no deeper. Life was lonely then. With no one to turn to for understanding, it all had to be kept inside.

There was a process of thinking in me that was frightening, a process that had begun at war. The question of whether I could perform at war was answered and was now added to my genetic human response system but controlled by social constraints. The relentless rage pounding inside my mind would create thoughts about going into the U.S. Capital and spraying machine gun fire into the Senate and Congress while screaming, "There, you assholes, see what it's like to face your own death and have your life vulnerable at any second? Now get in your goddamned chairs and either win the fucking war or end it, but do your job!" It seemed to me that the people still running the war had no concept that real lives were the price being paid; in their minds soldiers were objects in a game no more important than Checkers. As the military goes, these people in Washington struck me as a mediocre debate club in charge of running the rugby team.

I had no anger against war protesters who truly believed in their cause and little, if any, for those who went to Canada. But I wanted pure revenge on those whose self-centered egos had done anything to encourage the opposing forces to kill American soldiers. I would think of people who I felt should be taking the places in graves of those young soldiers who had died. How I despised them for having no sense of responsibility to the country but only to themselves and their self-serving egos! These thoughts were foreign to my rational thinking and I knew I would not act on them, yet I could not control their recurrence.

To this day, I am still surprised that no one else has acted on similar thoughts.

Nothing made me smile. I didn't want to do anything or go anywhere. No activity offered any interest. I was inert, a slug, and couldn't shake myself out of it. Society's values made no sense. I came to feel that young people had goals but older people who had once had comparable goals and achieved them, wondered where their lives had gone, and why their goals hadn't fulfilled their dreams. Now, later in life, they needed to find deeper meaning for their lives. I felt I was more like the older group than those my age. I knew I had to get out of that bar and out of that town, or I would be doomed to this wastefulness forever. I thought that if I could get away from it I might shock myself out of that lethargy. I had one dream left: the G.I. Bill. Maybe attending college would save me and reinforce the respectability of the facade to family and friends. This would at least appear reputable. It was the perfect idea all around. Nobody there would know me.

So began the physical running to escape myself mentally. I enrolled, was accepted, and then left for the university. Of course, it wasn't the salvation I'd hoped for. It would take years to accept that I could not run from myself. Emotions are like the tin cans attached to a newlywed's car, rattling and following wherever you go.

The facade now needed special attention. I pictured my outer self as a structure, like the outside of a house. Envision a beautiful house as my mental facade that was presented to the outside world. Built to protect the emotional hurt, the mental house I constructed was perfect. It was a huge mansion with beautiful white pillars; huge light-giving windows with well maintained flower boxes beneath each one. The front door was large and inviting with a polished brass handle and door knocker; the lapboard siding was bright white and freshly painted. The house was set on a large beautiful lot, perfectly manicured, with a lush green lawn. There were beautiful flowers of all types and colors, and lush red rose bushes climbing trellises at either side of the porch. It had a gently curving sidewalk flanked by lovely green, perfectly shaped bushes. And, of course, beautiful birds were singing gaily in the strong maple trees. Floating everywhere was the fragrance that soothes and forces one to stop, close one's eyes, inhale deeply and enjoy the wonderful pleasure of flowers.

Now climb the stairs to the porch and open the front door and enter the soul that the facade is disguising. You can sense that there had once been life here, but long, long ago. You meet a cold, clammy blue haze that raises goosebumps on your skin. The beautiful windows on the outside let in scant light; it is dark in the soul. Carpeting is worn, frayed and full of holes. The few pieces of furniture are broken. Gas pipes hiss and broken water valves overflow sinks and tubs, flooding the floor. Electric switches and outlets crackle and spew blue sparks. Chandeliers are crashed on the floor and doors hang on broken hinges. Stairs to the second floor are broken; plaster is cracked and strewn on the floors. The missing plaster exposes the cold wood slats behind, a hiding place for the most sad and bitter thoughts. Paint peels from what plaster remains, and there is a cold icy chill riding on a pungent, stale odor that riffles cobwebs everywhere. The air chokes you as you try to breathe.

This is where I allowed no one to enter. Having no skills to rebuild that interior, all my effort had to go into keeping the door between the inside and the outside tightly sealed. This took all my energy and left nothing for enjoyment of life, nor the ability to absorb new experiences. People who have suffered a traumatic event feel they have lost a part of their lives. Physically they exist, but mental and spiritual growth stops. All vitality is put toward maintaining the facade. I could not let my demolished interior be exposed to the world because I could not deal with it myself. The facade would sustain me for years before it began to fall apart. But there were years of grief, sadness, anger, heartbreak, anxiety, and hatred. Yet life was teaching me. This would become clear twenty years later.

My great dream to attend college, which had sustained me during the war, now seemed only an escape. It was a continuing heartbreak to be there yet unable to take advantage of the opportunities. I was running, and running had become my savior. Now I ran to new people, a new environment in which to hide, and within a short time of my arrival, new bars to visit. Because of my age, I was assigned a room in the graduate student dormitory. My roommate was from Pakistan and I liked him. There I was in a dormitory surrounded by rooms filled with graduate students from around the world. They all had ambitions and goals, anxious and deeply ambitious to study fifteen to twenty hours a day to achieve their goals to become doctors, cartographers, professors, businessmen, or scientists. These guys were going places with clear and focused minds, intent to complete advanced degrees. Then, filled with achievement and self-confidence, they would go off to live the goals for which they worked so hard. Their paths seemed well defined and organized; they knew exactly where they were taking their lives. It was torment for me to live there. All those guys knew what they wanted. They were the Cadillacs of the scholastic world, and here I had shown up on campus, a twenty-five -year-old rattling, broken down, rusted out machine on four flat tires. Recognizing my mind was not up to handing this opportunity, a different bitterness was added to my soul. My body had shown up but my mind was absent, away, still in the years gone by. The last dream was ending. I could see this dream and touch it, but the anguish of war's experience would not resolve itself, would not disappear and give me a clear mind to go on.

"Why can't I get back into life?" became my unanswered question. I had foolishly thought that the hard shell I had developed during war would naturally dissolve when I returned home. How wrong! The experience was so intense and the facade so crucial to existence, it did not disappear nor diminish when the threat was removed. It had now been four years since my return. Loud, sharp noises (doors slamming, cars backfiring) caused a startle response that was deeply and intensely from the time I was searching the jungle for danger. It was so entrenched that it had become natural to me. Before my mind realized the noise had been heard, my body had already ducked in defense. Now that is a great asset to survival while at war, but hardly needed at a birthday party in a small town in Wisconsin when a kid bursts a balloon. I remember when working on construction sites how the guys, in their loving way, would sneak up behind me and drop something flat on the plywood floor with a bang and I'd jump. It made them laugh and pleased them to no end. I've learned to laugh at that response. I think I laugh because it is so absurd to have learned something so intensely, so uncontrollably, and have it hang around for so many years.

One year, my brother and I dressed up and went to a New Year's party at a very popular, high-class hotel in downtown Milwaukee. Women were in evening gowns, swimming in jewelry, beautifully coiffed. Men were in suits or tuxedos and patent leather shoes. The hotel had a huge open atrium up to the top floors, each floor having a railed balcony. The party was on the main level, overlooked by the floors above. Everyone was merry, having a good time; hats, noisemakers and champagne were passed out at the appointed time. Just at the tick of midnight, the band played among cheers, hugs, Happy New Year everywhere. Amid the cheers and hoopla, hundreds of balloons floated down from overhead, as thick as a carpet. I was shocked. I knew what was coming. Elegantly dressed men and women, sufficiently giggly from cocktails, began displaying the children within themselves. High heels, cigars, hands, all were exploding balloons. Balloons were bursting everywhere; the sound was deafening, akin to gunshots. I was frozen in place and could not move. The thought that kept crossing my mind was, "If you only knew! If you only knew what humans do to humans!" This was one of many unsolicited thoughts I could not control. I gave a huge sigh of relief when it ended, then took a huge sip of whiskey to get my motor functions going.

There were other responses learned at war that I could not "unlearn." When walking down the street and passing a tree or alley way, I was always aware of the potential for someone to be hiding there. It is not that I was psychotic, actually believing someone was there; the vigilance needed to stay alive in the jungle was so intense and constant that my subconscious never gave up the self-defense behaviors. The intensity of those experiences did not diminish. There were other residues of war that became habit. I don't celebrate my birthday. It is easy for me to recognize that for what it is: guilt for surviving when others did not. The learned behavior of never carrying keys or lots of coins that create a jingling in my pocket because someone might hear me coming and set an ambush still resides. I don't like people close behind me. It took years to be comfortable in places like movie theaters. In fact, I am still not that comfortable. I will not sit with my back to a doorway. There are other oddities I attribute to war experience, but the main point is that I learned not to trust others. I gave up trying to erase these from memory as "needed" responses. I just accept them and thank Mark Twain for teaching me to laugh at myself.

I cannot communicate strongly enough the effects of emotional trauma. It does not exist as a half-hour lingering thought after a bad dream. It is the continuation of a nightmare becoming real and it is there every day, every week and every year after year after year, until that wound is soothed. Maybe, if it can be. There has not been one day in thirty years that has passed without my having been aware of the experience of war more than half my life ago.

FRANTICALLY RUNNING FROM MYSELF

CHAPTER SEVEN

The university was a great place to hide and so I hid there for two years, taking classes that sounded interesting. I had no particular professional goal. My goal was to hide. I was just there, faking my way through life, holding on to the facade but so lost in society. I just could not make sense out of what had once been great dreams. They no longer existed and I knew I would fail at college. I recall everyone so intent on classes and homework, their hearts and souls into their lives and dreams. I just did not fit and I would think, again and again, "If you only knew." Because of my experiences of war, I knew things they did not. I was the odd man out.

So while the grad students were intent on classes and goals, I wandered the university as an alien. I did well at classes I liked, mostly math or science. Classes that I found boring I dropped or just let lapse into poor grades. I honestly just didn't care about those failures. How sad to let such opportunities just skip by. Nights found the grads at the library and me at the bars. I was alone, lost and to myself, anesthetizing that coldness deep inside with alcohol. Many days I'd just walk the campus, avoid class, or walk downtown. I was always alone and lonely for something; I just didn't know what. I felt I had to stay at the university because it made the facade respectable to family and friends back home. But this cover up would eventually begin to lose its effect. It was too painful to maintain. I am to this day sad that I lost that dream of college.

On the other hand, there were a few experiences during my college days that were enjoyable, and some very educational in an odd way. Science was extremely interesting; I was introduced to a fundamental law of science, hypothesis, which states that an idea is always possible until it is proven, factually, to be an impossibility. One morning, I was sitting in a genetics class studying the different eye color possibilities by the combination of different genes, i.e., if a male parent had blue eyes and a mother had brown eyes, what are the different possibilities for an offspring to have blue eyes and the possibilities of brown? The professor was in front of the class; discussion was drifting here and there, and then landed on the topic of God and life. The professor straightened his posture and, in what he must have felt was the most enlightened statement he could present, said point blank and arrogantly, "There is no God." In no way was he putting this up for discussion or rebuttal; he was stating a fact! I was shocked. Not just that he was arrogant enough to think that as an intellectual he had reached the pinnacle of knowledge, and that he could perfectly explain this extraordinary thing called life. But in his shameless arrogance, he had broken the rules that his own profession found to be fundamental. Anything was possible until it could be positively proven impossible! I wanted to confront him, but didn't.

That incident taught me a great deal. I became constantly annoyed at how arrogantly many other professors held that belief. These are the people studying on the frontiers of the issues and discoveries of life, but find life no more of a marvel than to make definitive conclusions and give impressions that they have the knowledge and understanding of existence. Science also states that less than 50 percent of the brain's function is understood. If so, how could anyone claim to have the answers to life? What if the answers are all in the 50 percent or more that is yet to be discovered? What if we were to perfectly understand 99 percent of the brain and the answer lies in the last 1 percent? This intellectual thinking about God and life, while upsetting then, would be valuable at a crisis time for me years later. No education is wasted.

It was typical to take one easy course each semester to reduce the stress. I registered for a class titled "History of Symphony" and thought it would be a breeze: fifty minutes of listening to music, which would be time to sleep or study for other classes. However, I was wrong. It was a tough course and demanded fifty minutes of attention during class, but the results were profound. I found not just the beauty of classical music, but I found Mozart (or he found me). What a gift to someone who had never been introduced to classical music! So when Mozart spoke to me and said, "Make whatever you want of this," I could not attach any of the dark feelings I had to his music. He did not belong in my soul as it was. So powerful was the beauty of his music that I could not deny it and had to come out of the anger and float on the strings of violins that I still float on today.

Even with Mozart, my inability to live deeper than the facade made college life impossible to maintain beyond the first two years. I was not able to focus on classes, was always feeling alone. The university was no longer the great hiding place it had been. I was failing my last dream. I just did not fit, and if I did not fit there, then where? I was alone in a society that held nothing for me. Its goals seemed empty and materialistic. A car, or house could not restore my happiness? These were the thoughts that continually crossed my mind as healthy goals for life, but they did not work for me. Why did I not want these things? I had no answer. I was getting anxious to move on, go some place, but I had nowhere to go. I was desperate; the facade had to be kept up. It was all I had left.

One day, while walking around instead of attending classes, I was full of anxiety, knowing that my stay at college was nearly over. Running to college had not helped quiet my restlessness. I needed to run again, to escape this society. While mulling this over, I was startled out of my thinking by a magnificent poster displaying the continent of Africa along with the inviting words, "The toughest job you'll ever love! Join the Peace Corps." My whole body swelled, my mind seemed awakened to hope. A place to go, to escape! I felt the poster had been put in that window just waiting for me, and so was Africa. As a child, pictures in *National Geographic* - especially the remote people and cultures of Africa - had fascinated me. How incredible that these cultures existed somewhere on the earth! As a child, Africa was as far as a distant planet, something I saw in photographs and could only dream of. To go there was foolish thinking and remained in the realm of fascination.

But as an adult, I had been to the other side of the world, had lived and survived in the jungles there. I had slept many nights on the jungle floor, clearing a small sleeping spot of leaves and twigs, not just for comfort but to assure that in my sleep I did not snap a twig and give away our position to those looking to kill us. We had slept under the relentless monsoon rains, soaked to the bone and beyond, shivering in the morning mist until the sun warmed us. There had been the jungle rot melting the skin of my ankles, creating another battle. How many times had we slept near a recently used trail and set up a claymore mine with trip wire to ambush any poor soul that passed in the night? How disgusting it was to have my final thoughts at night be of that poor soul trotting through the jungle, and in one step going from his dream of home and loved ones to the everlasting. I felt sad and ashamed that I could find no better reason for this than that we didn't want to die any more than he did. So, how could the jungles of Africa scare me? I had also seen the spectacular beauty of the wildlife in those Vietnamese jungles, but could never pay full attention to them, so maybe, I would enjoy them in Africa. I knew that I could be on a plane and over the continent of Africa in a night. And, if I slept on the plane, how would time or distance matter?

Without hesitation, I hurried into the Peace Corps office. I felt a sense of salvation, something that put a flicker of hope in my worn out soul. I spoke to the woman there, was given the general expectations of the Peace Corps, and a large catalog to look through. The catalog was a listing of countries and projects around the world that were in need of volunteers. I was so focused on Africa that I never considered a look at South America, Asia, or anywhere else. I went directly to openings in Africa and then directly to projects in the equatorial rain forest – the jungle. For the first time in years I felt a sensation of hope, and happiness reach behind the facade and put warmth inside me. I was excited; it was like getting a sip of water in the desert after crawling days in the sand. My soul felt "something" and it felt good!

The Peace Corps held several great opportunities for me. First, it was an enormous salvation for the facade. It would beautify that image before the world and my family. Second, it was a new chance. I had been with the human race when they were destroying human life; this was a chance for me to balance my mental scales and do something to help the human race, to put love in the world, not hatred and killing.

At the time it seemed curious that when I was given that catalog of Peace Corps projects, I went not just to Africa, but also straight to countries in the jungle; most of Africa is desert and grassland. It looked as if I had known to pick the jungle, like a long-held dream that had already been mapped out in my subconscious. I guess I must have thought about this very deeply as I had no fear, no second-guessing, never an apprehension about Africa. I had endured the jungles of Vietnam so I had no fear of living in the African jungle, just a deepening fascination about the cultures. An adventure with this magnitude seemed to have an effect strong enough to rouse my soul to life. I was energized! I signed up.

With great excitement and anticipation, yet the sad realization that a college degree was not to be, I closed up shop at the university. I did not belong there anyway, as I had come to realize. It was not my mind that needed an education, but my soul that needed to be rebuilt. However, it did hurt deeply to fail there. I had needed to maintain the façade during the months needed to process the paperwork for the Peace Corps, The first new goal since coming home sustained me.

The date of departure was set, my plane ticket was issued, and I was on my way. When I left the coast of the U.S., I looked back with a feeling similar to that I'd had when leaving Vietnam, though not as severe. There was a sense that I was flying out of a very bad experience where all dreams had failed, and I was now heading to new ones. I took the famous Pan Am flight from Boston that hopped along the west coast of Africa and stopped at all the capital cities: Dakar, Conakry, Freetown, Monrovia, Abidjan, Accra, Cotonou, Lagos, Doula, and finally deposited me in Libreville, Gabon. The year was 1976.

PART TWO
AFRICA: FROM DREAM
TO REALITY

As a young boy, I was fascinated with the cultures of Africa shown in the photographs in *National Geographic* magazines. I remember lying on my bed with legs crossed at the ankles and hands folded behind my head, dreaming of the exotic cultures. Although I understood that America and Africa existed on the same planet, Africa seemed infinitely distant. I felt an invisible veil between the two cultures, a veil I could not pass through; I could only dream of that strange life on the other side. Then, I was only a mental traveler. Although I could not have realized it at the time, these images would help me, when later added to my Vietnam War jungle experiences, to relish the collision of cultures.

WAR WON'T LEAVE ME ALONE

CHAPTER EIGHT

It was nighttime when I arrived in Gabon. The unforgettable blast of heat and smells that met me in the door of the plane was both the same and different from when I first arrived in Vietnam. The scents in Vietnam were scorching air mixed with jet fuel. In contrast, the airport in Africa was near the ocean, and the hot air seemed stilled by the scent of flowers mixed with ocean breeze. I was immediately in love; the intrigue so powerfully pulling me in, I could give no resistance.

The next morning I saw Africa for the first time. There were modern buildings flanked by mud shacks - a ghetto mixed with the modern world. Suits and ties mixed with bare feet and traditional dress. Cars traveling alongside carts pulled by hand. The haves and the have-nots, the stark rich and the stark poor, all mingled together. Everywhere there was the music, the beautiful music that is only in Africa: a mixture of instruments I was not accustomed to hearing- udu, djembe, doum doum, bougarabou and kora-blending together in an almost unearthly harmony, and constant sounds of drums!

The intrigue and fascination of Africa would quiet my anxiety-ridden soul. Not heal it, but calm it. There was so much to see, to learn. I was deeply fascinated with this new experience that for the time being it relieved the gnawing of past preoccupations. It was probably only this extraordinary adventure that could have excited me beyond the focus of war. Africa would be a therapy long and desperately hoped for: It created a balance in my mind and soul.

I was absorbing Africa and soon I would be going deeper into the interior, away from all modern conveniences; leaving centuries behind. My project was to build a school in the most rural, isolated area of the country, deep in the jungle. I would also be responsible for training and transferring building trade skills to four local men who would then train others. The school would provide the chance for the children there to learn to read, which I consider to be the most important and enjoyable of all scholastic skills. They would also learn math and science, but they could do no other studies without reading. This may seem insignificant in America, but visualize a place where no one has seen a book or understands its purpose. Now think about how the world would open up to them when they learned to read! Books have always been great friends and teachers for me; I would never have come to Africa if I had not been able to read about the place as a young child. I was proud and excited to be a part of what I was told President Bongo was doing for his country of Gabon; providing schools and hospitals for remote peoples. I felt I was helping to make the world a better place and genuinely balance the destruction I had participated in while in Vietnam.

There were sixteen volunteers in our group. We were to be sent in pairs to different villages around the country to build these schools. But first, we had to learn the language. Gabon was a former French colony so the national language was French. We were sent to Bangui, the capital of the Central African Republic for an immersion course in French and cultural studies. We spent our days in formal French classes and the evenings on the town plying our French on the friendly people of the capital city, absorbing the culture. The people of Central Africa were very warm and it was fun engaging them in simple conversations. This gave us all good laughs. I enjoyed the street vendors who sold their many wares, and especially the Capitaine fish they caught in the Ubangi River and grilled fresh right there on the streets, seasoned hot and unforgettably delicious. Sold and wrapped in old papers, the fish were eaten with our fingers. I loved the smells, the ever-present African music, and the beautiful colors of dress.

While in Bangui I witnessed two amazing events. On a sweltering hot day millions upon millions of locusts swarmed in, blanketing the ground and darkening the sky. It was eerie to see such an impressive act of nature. I had heard of these locust swarms and how they devoured every bit of green growth, leaving barren fields and starving populations, but I had not heard about what I witnessed that day. This memory remains one of the most incredible mental images of human desperation. Starving people of all ages, children and adults, scrambled everywhere and in every gymnastic manner to snatch those locusts out of the air. Some ate them raw as they caught them; others collected them as if picking cotton and put them in sacks. Still others skewered them on sticks and roasted them over open fires. The people were devouring the locusts that had come in swarms to devour their food source. What did I really have to complain about in life?

The second event rivals the greatest human tragedy I have ever witnessed. Jean-Bedel Bokassa was the President of the Central African Republic, one of the poorest nations in the world. I was in Bangui within several yards of him as he passed in his presidential limo followed by a procession of his personal bodyguards hanging out of every door and window of their cars. They were brandishing sub-machine guns, impressive to the locals but a sight out of the Keystone Cops for me. I could see his face clearly and noticed it lacked something, I wasn't sure what. It was cold, purely cold. This public appearance was the preliminary to his declaration of himself as Emperor

Bokassa the First, emulating his hero Napoleon. The coronation and celebrations cost somewhere around 200 million dollars, about 25 percent of the gross national product of that country for one year. He later bankrupted the country and in only two years was ousted from power but not before massacring one hundred school children. The story goes that those children had not purchased their school uniforms from a company that either Bokassa owned or that used his cotton material. Their decapitated heads were found in his deep freeze, and there was talk of cannibalism. He managed, like all cowards, to flee the country. He was later tried and convicted of the massacre but not of cannibalism.

It was there in Africa that I was made aware of the phenomenon of ruthless leaders who dealt in torture, murder, extermination of their own or rival cultures, and the financial rape of their own countrymen. And when the population got smart and turned on these dictators, most fled the country to cowardly exile. It has always amazed me how some men climb to power and abuse their own people so horrendously, ordering their henchmen to commit indescribable atrocities. But when they are faced with what they dealt out, they run and hide in fear. Idi Amin did this in Uganda after slaughtering thousands of political foes. The Shah of Iran ran, Sese Seko in Zaire fled, and Marcos in the Philippines raped the country, publicly thumbed his nose, and saved his own butt and the millions of dollars he stole. There was Pinochet in Chile; Romanian Ceausescu and his wife, Elena, ran but were caught and hanged on Christmas Eve for the abuse of their people. Baby Doc Duvalier pillaged his country of Haiti, murdered many, then fled and lives in luxury in France. Pol Pot in Cambodia is yet another example. All in my lifetime, and there are more. How these people get so many others to commit their crimes and then flee with the purse is something I will never understand. Why do so many follow these mad men and women? What is their power? Do we allow those in power in the U.S. to get away with similar things and follow the leader in events such as the Vietnam War? Could it be that the majority can accept these things as long as they feel secure at home?

I have come to believe that history will find those of the U.S. Government in power during the years of the Vietnam War to have been similar cowards, incapable of taking responsibility for the killings of that war. They were unable to comprehend that lives (not their own) on both sides were being lost every hour that they procrastinated, pondered and pontificated. Had they understood the horrors that were taking place, if they had been sent to the killing fields, I think they would have stopped that war and negotiated night and day to end it. No doubt if their lives had been at risk that war would have ended much more quickly.

There was one other happening that I found reprehensible. The Central African professors, some European educated, were delightful, warm, enthusiastic and intelligent instructors. In class they were effective, and on the streets they were great representatives of their cultures. I was in fascination of all their teachings. But when asked a question about politics and government, one of the professors stopped moving, his eyes widened and a cold look of fear swept over him. "Don't ask me about those things, you can't ask those things!" he whispered. For the rest of the night, that professor was not the same; an uneasy sorrow came over me as the atmosphere turned quiet. The volunteers were confronted by the Peace Corps director who explained that we were not to ask these people any questions about politics, not in any way, and especially not about President Bokassa. They could be arrested and disappear along with their entire families. Freedom of speech is not a universal value. In fact, these fanatical dictators seemed so deeply intimidated by political foes and intellectuals who might expose their treachery, that these were the first opponents to be found floating down rivers or otherwise quieted. I could not comprehend how these decent people could live in this constant fear of death, and I felt deeply for them. Again I was made aware of a profound sadness and shame in the human race. I felt so deeply sorry for these wonderful people and grew to despise Bokassa. Would the abuse these people suffered under the control of their leader have been a cause for war? Is there a cause for which it is worth fighting a war? I would ask myself these questions many times in the future.

THE BEAUTY WAS SOOTHING

CHAPTER NINE

We left the Central African Empire which we had entered when it was the Central African Republic, and went back to the equally warm and friendly people of Gabon. We were now ready for our assignments and relocation to our new homes deep in the jungle villages. Our group, having lost several volunteers to cultural shock, was now of an odd number. The director, and to this day I am not sure if I was being asked or told, assigned me to a village by myself. He knew my background at war and assumed I would survive well enough on my own. Luckily, he was right. I was just as excited as before; this assignment diminished nothing, and only heightened the intrigue. I was issued a new four-wheel-drive Toyota, a diesel powered bush truck that was as powerful as it was beautiful. When it was packed with my one suitcase of personal things, a few jerry cans of extra diesel fuel, a good supply of water, a shortwave radio, a few other necessary items, and the name of my new home village and road directions, I slid the transmission into first gear and headed for the "heart of darkness."

Seldom does the English language leave me without words to express a feeling or sensation, but this was one of those occasions. When I departed the blacktop road of Libreville for the first time and hit the single lane, dirt road on a journey of hundreds of miles into a world I had only imagined, I sensed I was being cured of all the anger, hatred, guilt, shame, confusion, and misery of what had come before. I was heading into hope and a new chance at life. I had no words to describe how deeply grateful I was.

The drive took several days, with a first night stop in a small village, home to an American English teacher. She was isolated, loved what she was doing, but was happy to see and speak to someone from home. We shared our enthusiastic excitement of Africa in a long conversation that night. Back on the road the next day I headed for Lastoursville to another sleep over. Then on towards my new home. Along the way I would cross south over the equator, and then over the great Ogouee River. It was the dry season and the roads were passable. I would drive this road many times in the next several years, and be forever appreciative that my first experience was not in the rainy season when the trip could have taken weeks. Waiting for the dry season makes the journey possible. The only drawback to these roads in the dry season was a phenomenon called washboarding. Water flow, during the rains turned the road surface into something resembling an old washboard with tiny waves closely spaced together. It was like ripples on a lake, but this was hard clay. The washboarding would go on for 30 to 50 miles. The effect was to rattle a truck, its contents, and especially the driver unforgivably. When I would stop for a break, my body kept on rattling, like sea legs after getting off a boat.

That first drive was purely majestic and romantic. The sky, the endless jungle and what I knew it hid were more beautiful than I had anticipated. I remembered how unrealistically beautiful home had become in my mind while in Vietnam, and how disappointed I was to find it just as when I left. I must have been dreaming of Africa then, for here was that beauty before me now. An occasional tiny village would pop up every couple of hours and the barefoot villagers, young and old, and mothers holding babies in their arms, would race to the edge of the road and wave enthusiastically. I'd wave and smile back as I passed, leaving a long cloud of dust hanging in the air. I got the impression that I had just given them the most excitement to come their way in a long time. Travelers were scarce and life was typically slow and confined to an isolated world. I thought I must be to them what witnessing the launch of the Space Shuttle would be for me. Most of these folks had seen trucks, but knew nothing of the experience of being in one.

Dusty, tired, and bones rattling, I arrived in Lastoursville at the home of two Peace Corps volunteers who were just finishing their two years of working on a school. In the Army, one of the first questions people from the same country a long way from home ask each other is, "Where ya from?" I was surprised to hear this same question from one of the volunteers. I told him I was from Wisconsin. "No kidding! What city?" he asked, to which I answered Milwaukee. "I'm from Madison!" he exclaimed. There in the middle of the jungles of Africa was a guy who grew up only 90 miles from me. This fellow Wisconsinite was Dick Steeper and I would come to know him as one of the most intelligent men I have ever met. He, his partner, and I spoke of home, life in Africa and the time they had spent there. They entertained me with food, well-appreciated beer and great conversation. Their love of Africa was obvious and I felt I was in the right place at exactly the right time. Dick loved Africa so much that he had already hired on to stay in the country with a private company. Africa was in his blood, too.

I slept great that night; it was a new sleep that was not haunted by war. I fell asleep dreaming of the new home and neighbors I would meet the next day deeper into the jungle. Awaking early, thanking Dick for the hospitality, and eager to get on the road, I set out for Koula Moutou, the final stop before my arrival in Lebangy. The jungle had lost none of its intrigue while I slept. The last couple of hours on the road were as romantic as any previous. Although I was aware that all I was really seeing was the wall of jungle trees that lined that dirt road, my mind knew what lay behind them, and romanced those thoughts. At times I would wonder if a mighty gorilla had its eyes on me as I passed, or how many deadly serpents were part of all the other spectacular life watching me? What about the Pygmies? Were they seeing me pass, curious to see the noisemaker, but too timid to expose themselves? I wanted to meet them, but knew from research that because of being poorly regarded by outsiders, they tended to avoid contact. Not just the arrogant French colonists but many of the Africans thought the Pygmies a lower form of life. As a white man, I knew they would certainly not have enough trust to expose their beloved rain forest to me. Having experienced this lack of trust in the human race, I felt a distant brotherhood with them. These powerful and quixotic thoughts captivated me.

I finally recognized Koula Moutou only by its size, as there were no road signs or rest stops. The map I was given was as valuable as those the military had given us in Vietnam. If lucky, the maps were accurate enough to let you know what hemisphere you were in. The exceptional ones might tell you what country. Beyond that, they were simply pretty little brochures whose markings had no counterparts on the globe. So in Africa, I was on my own. The villages I had passed were tiny with a couple of small dirt homes but Koula Moutou was much bigger; it seemingly popped out of the jungle. Its narrow quarter mile of blacktop was definite proof that I had arrived. That stretch of smooth road was relief to my shaken body. Just the name Koula Moutou was romantic, but now I was standing on a hillside, looking down on this town I had only read about. I could see it, smell it and hear it! I could see the life and the people there; it was real! The place did exist! And there, running through the center, I could see the great Ogouee River. What god was I to thank for this spectacular experience that was certainly not of my making? I marveled, as I did many times in Africa, at the majesty of life; the realization that life was much bigger than we are; that life is about more than any one of us, and greater than any single person. This realization eventually led me beyond my egocentric concentration on my war experiences, and helped me choose between going inward to my own demons, or moving outwards to experience life as a part, not the center. This thought frightened me for it put the decision in my hands; I was responsible for what I added to life, not just what I took from it. And there could be no excuses except those I might create to avoid responsibility to this much greater purpose. When I recognized this beautiful alternate choice in life, I realized how ashamed of myself I would be not to participate in a way to do my part in making life better. I would slowly come to recognize that the evil emotions or feelings that were the result of war were nothing more than my confrontation with the human race, my life, my anger, and how I had taken it all personally. I realized I had an alternative, which was an honest acceptance of the imperfection and disappointment experienced in all humankind.

Africa offered proof that life was much bigger than just the human element. I had been locked in a battle of wasted time, living in my little ego with my anger, my depression, my shame, my guilt, my hatred, my hurt, my fear, my, my, my! All had been about me! While locked in that egocentric world, I could not see the larger life view. I didn't appreciate the birds, the trees, the flowers, and the goodness in the world. So the choice became so clear to me, either stay locked in that ego, not grow in life, be miserable and add that misery to the world, or surrender that ego, and be an asset to life, not a deficit. Words like forgiveness, acceptance, and courage to move on began to replace those useless feelings that had me frozen in a time long past and filled with misery. But here before me was God's cure offered if I chose to take it. I chose the better, and it soothed me. The birds, floral life, and spectacular animal life became the images I kept within, replacing the darkness. Fascinations that had been lost in that war's madness were exploding to life again, and I had no time to ask where they had been. I had no choice but to be impressed and see my own smallness in the world. I was also made aware of my own importance in a new view of life that asked only that I do my part, put away that which needed to be put away in my soul, and accept that I am part of human life, imperfect as it is, and get moving.

When I first arrived in Koula Moutou, I reported to the prefect - the mayor- who had been informed of my purpose. After greeting me warmly, completing formalities, he said in paternal fashion while smiling, "Make sure and find a woman, it's important!" Not knowing how else to respond, I laughed. He had taken me completely by surprise – who thought politicians would talk like this? However, I immediately appreciated his honesty and knew I had met a man who spoke the truth and was to be respected. He was someone whom I would come to know and respect further for his leadership and compassion for his people. He shook my hand, wished me well and most importantly made me feel genuinely welcomed. He could not have known that at the moment I had what I considered many more important things on my mind than a woman. It still makes me smile today in remembering the exchange that left me thinking, what about this woman stuff here in Africa? The subject had crossed my mind and I had wondered about this, but I had always left that question alone, not knowing how to answer it. Now the time to think of it was apparently near, and yet I still had only curiosity. I was on some other wavelength, fascinated by Africa. I felt those things would take care of themselves; there was too much else to think of. I had certainly not come to Africa to find a woman. Eventually, I would come to see how sex was just beneath the open surface of human interaction in Africa. Disguised at home in the US, but quite apparent and acceptable in this country.

I made a short inspection of Koula Moutou to familiarize myself with where I would be buying supplies, where the small French hospital was, and just to get a sense of the place. I was surprised and happy to find that an old Greek businessman had opened a small Boulangerie where several times a week a limited amount of fresh French bread was sold. This would become a highly anticipated treat. Every week I'd be there to get a loaf just out of the oven and eat it hot right on the spot. I never had the self-control to let it sit for long on the seat of the truck before pulling pieces off to nibble on. The smell and taste were just too divine. I loved taking fresh loaves back for my new neighbors; the kids especially raced to get their portion.

Departing Koula Moutou for Lebangy, I swung the truck out and headed south on the last section of road toward the Congo. I would be going close but not into that country, but how could I not be purely thrilled to even think I was close to this country that carried the name Congo? Besides Egypt, this had to be the most recognizable name in all of Africa, and what great adventure stories and history had come from that place!

The road was now narrower, and the jungle canopy closed off the sky. No longer a connecting road between major cities, it was poorly maintained with centuries old log bridges. I passed small villages, and as always the children would flock to the side of the road to hoot, holler, and dance about as I passed, while the older folks looked on from deeper in the village. Later, I realized that these folks might only see a truck pass every couple of weeks, months in the rainy season, and this was always an exciting spectacle for them. Most had never even touched the metal of a truck, much less been in one. Many did not understand the concept of glass, and that it could not be talked through.

As I drove on, there was the realization that I left the last bit of western influence behind me. People wore no shoes and the common dress was a simple piece of cloth wrapped around the body. For women, it was tucked in above the breast; for men, tied around the back of the neck. I recognized early on that the women were the workhorses here. I passed them walking the road carrying loads that bent them over. They had the most remarkable woven baskets on their backs that were supported by a woven strap that came around the forehead and was carried by the strength of the neck. These were undoubtedly their shopping baskets. Goats and chickens had freedom to roam the villages as they pleased, and I would learn that you best not hit one or you would be in for the confrontation of your life. Usually this confrontation would only resolve itself when the owner was paid an inflated value. The generally accepted understanding was that all westerners were by birth very wealthy and should spread a bit of that wealth around.

I worried that I might overshoot my intended village and end up peering into the eyes of the Congolese border guards. Americans were not welcomed in the Congo. This was an ally of Cuba, and the inhabitants had assumed the dislike of us as they were told to. I was not keen on the idea of disappearing this early in my visit to Africa. So, I stopped periodically and asked, "Where is Lebangy?" Children always rushed to circle the truck and stared at me with great curious eyes. The more courageous would touch the truck. The older villagers were more guarded, and a man would generally approach first to inspect me. Consequently, I would learn there were two worlds there in the bush; one inhabited by the people familiar with the French colonists, and another filled with those who came after the French departure. Those familiar with the French despised them and some were afraid of them. The French had been ruthless, selfish colonists who made these people suffer in many ways. I would later (after the people's acceptance of me) hear some of these stories and be ashamed for humankind. It took months for me to prove myself different from those "whites" and be accepted. This would indeed become my biggest challenge, but also the one from which I received the greatest rewards, especially from the children. And God be thanked for the curious, open minds of these wonderful children who bring joy, love and laughter to the world, keeping it in balance.

AFRICA WELCOMES ME HOME

CHAPTER TEN

"La bas," "Lebangy la bas, that way!" Well I knew it was "that way" but how many villages, how much farther? Every child wanted to be the one with the answer, and in his or her enthusiasm I understood it to be the village after the next river. "Okay, merci!" I repeated in one village after another.

I was never the least bit apprehensive in approaching Lebangy, nor did I experience any fear. My sense of calm came in part from my past experiences in Vietnam. There, we had routinely entered villages in search of Vietcong soldiers. Our reception in those villages was always icy. The people showed, by expression and communication, that they neither wanted us there nor were going to give a bit of information. They would just stand there with blank, cold expressions. My reception in Africa had already proved a world apart from that coldness. The extended length of time in Vietnam confronting constantly the possibility of my own death could never be matched. Today, I may be scared of something but it is so incomparable to war that it simply does not register as fear.

I crossed the log bridge, over the river and was there. This was it, Lebangy. The tiny village was laid out in a large circle; the road passed through the center and in all directions the village was surrounded by the magnificent green jungle, one of the greatest concentrations and diversity of life on the planet. As I had been hyper sensitive in the jungles of Vietnam, so was I now. Every part of my vision, sense of smell and hearing was alive. The difference was that this time it was out of joyful excitement. The barefoot children had started chasing the truck on arrival, and continued until I stopped in the middle of the village. They immediately inspected the truck, looked at it from all angles and peered through the open windows as American children might have peered into a space shuttle cockpit. These children were a delight of energy and endless curiosity and I could see in their eyes that nothing would excite them more than a chance to jump up in the bed of the truck, or more incredibly, to sit inside, so I let them do both. In squeals of excitement they raced, pushing and shoving to be first. The elder men approached cautiously, the women stayed in the background, the curiosity of childhood long ago replaced with the cautiousness of maturity.

Africans who were too young to have experienced the French were more open to me. There was a distinct division in the culture and it was obvious that the elders wanted no part of the French, their language, their fashions, etc., while the younger were drawn to the new information that was reaching them as the outside world became more accessible. The older villagers had only their African names in their native Njebi language, while the younger had their African names and a trailing western name. I witnessed two different social behaviors mingling together to produce a tear in the culture, one hanging onto the past, and one advancing into the future.

Confident of my French, I began to introduce myself. A few sentences into this well practiced introduction, I was jolted out of my excitement by the realization that these people didn't speak French. They had no idea what I was saying. Nothing but blank stares answered me. There was no sound as neighbor snuck cautious glances at neighbor as if to ask, "Who the heck is he and what the heck is he doing here?" I wondered if they would dash off to collect weapons and return to rid the village of an evil Frenchman, for to them all whites were Frenchman and all Frenchman evil.

At that particular moment I could do little to hide that I was a white man. I was now standing deep in the African jungle with no means of communication. Had I thought things out better, I might have expected this. After all I had come there to build a school so the children could learn to read, write and speak French. This was the bush; these people would have had neither language training nor a desire to speak the language of a people they detested. Schools had never been part of their life; their language and their traditions were what were important to them. It had gotten them through the centuries and would do fine for those to come. After a short lull, I was saved by some of the younger children who had received some schooling and came forward to interpret. As more curious villagers approached, I was delighted to find more who spoke some very broken French, at least enough to get by on.

When the villagers finally understood who I was and what I was there for, things improved quickly. I met the chief, who was barefoot, and clad only in a cloth wrapped round him. I was introduced around, and smiles began to emerge as these kind people had a hard time and good laughs trying to pronounce my name. "Myeke" was the closest they came and it was settled on. This made me happy, for only minutes before I had thoughts that I might have to get in my truck and return to Koula Moutou in a hurry, fleeing angry African villagers competing for my hide. I received constant, warm attention through that day and late into the night as people came to view this new white apparition in their village. I settled into the house they chose for me, which was the finest in the village and belonged to the chief. It was mud-walled, tin-roofed, had a dirt floor, a rough sawn door to the front, another one to the back, and two small wood plank windows. An outhouse was where those things are supposed to be. The house offered no other amenities, although it did have fresh running water, unfortunately it was running in a streambed up in the mountains. Regardless, it was refreshing and the purest water I would ever taste. Just beyond that back door, only a few yards away, was the jungle. Over the years many visitors would come from behind that first wall of trees to cause my neighbors and me no end of frantic welcomes. I would spend much time in that jungle of wonders, in constant awe of life there. I would absorb the teaching I received from the villagers on how to exist there, how to communicate with the animals, what to do if confronted by a gorilla or an elephant or the many serpents and vipers, what could be safely eaten as well as what would eat me, where to find water when none seemed near, and if lost, how to watch the monkeys and eat what they ate. I would learn how to hunt like the best of the villagers (though I must admit, I did all my hunting with a camera, but they let me hang with them anyway).

I would have been foolish not to see and finally understand just how beautifully these people existed with nature. My travels through *National Geographic* had always left me wondering how people could possibly live there and raise families, neighbors to the many deadly vipers and the great variety of deadly animals. I witnessed over and over until I came to a deep understanding that they did not control nor try to control anything; they simply lived as part of the land, respecting it and knowing how to coexist with it. And I knew that somewhere out there, somewhere in that great natural cathedral of life were the caretakers of the forest, the Pygmies. If this was not heaven, it was its suburb. There was a part of me that felt there might indeed be a bit of spirituality left in me, and if so, I had to humbly believe that God was guiding me on a fascinating, educational tour of it, telling me, "It's not all about you and not all about humans. There is something much greater; let's find out if you can see it." I saw it! And would continue to see it there in one of the greatest universities in the world!

NEW TEACHERS -
NEW MEANING IN LIFE

CHAPTER ELEVEN

Living in Lebangy, Gabon, remains one of the most intense learning periods in my life. Not a day passed without intrigue, adventure and fascination. Large cities of Africa are modern, with citizens as unfamiliar and intimidated by the bush as anyone born and raised in New York City. But the bush was the "home" I was looking for. So complete was my fascination, the stay soothed the devastated soul I'd dragged back from Southeast Asia.

During the time I was there, Lebangy had a population of about seventy-five; there were no census records, so this is my best guess. The houses were mud walled with tin or grass roofs and dirt floors. The interior of the huts was simple. Partition walls of mud had no doors, save for a piece of cloth for privacy; there was no electricity or plumbing. The inhabitants never spoke of those modern conveniences, didn't plan or dream of them; most had never experienced them. The houses formed a perimeter around an open central area cut out of the jungle which reflected a centuries old defensive position against attack from the outside and protection from the great wild animals and reptiles. The area around the perimeter was both beautiful and fatal. It didn't pay to be careless except in deadly dividends.

I will always be stunned that one part of the world remains unchanged, while another part changes so rapidly that some live in a society that is constantly becoming obsolete and being replaced with "bigger and better." I don't understand it; I only know that going into the bush of Africa was a leap back in time for me. I stepped back centuries in medicine, science, education, religion, music, food preparation, clothing and footwear (or lack of it), women's make up, fashion, male-female interactions, relationships and more. Belief in medical healing was one area where my culture and the culture of Lebangy collided in a memorable way.

We were in the monsoon season, which brought endless days of downpour with spectacular thunder and lightning. The dry, hard packed clay of the dry season now became thick, oozing, slippery mud. The small log bridges over streams would wash out and we would be cut off from the world for weeks or months before repairs could be made. My four-wheel drive bush truck was no match for this mud. Even walking was difficult and exhausting in mud that refused to give your feet back.

Sleeping during the monsoon in a house with nothing to insulate against the endless drone pounding the roof was unnerving at first. To sleep was impossible; to be heard in conversation one had to yell. It was like living under a waterfall. But over time it became a soothing noise, and provided tranquil sleep. And it provided a place out of the rain, unlike Vietnam where we had slept on the ground in the mud under those tremendous monsoon storms with no protection overhead. I think this made me feel that I had moved up a neighborhood to a higher class and was grateful for the comforts. I knew how bad it could be.

It was late in such a night when I was awakened by a sound in the distance. It turned out to be a pounding on my front door, less than 15 feet from me, the sound dimmed dramatically by the rain. I flung back the wisp of my mosquito net, and lit a kerosene lamp on my way to the door. There stood Tsumbu. He was drenched, with rivers of water running down his body.

I quickly motioned him in. Tsumbu was a neighbor and had become a good friend. He looked about my age, but no records were kept in our village, so I couldn't be sure. Tsumbu was the nephew of the chief, and next in line to fill that role. He was intelligent and respected; a gentle man who loved to laugh with great animation at himself and life. This was a great quality and a good example for me, the serious war veteran. Tsumbu spoke broken French and was my interpreter to the older villagers who spoke only Njebi. He had taught me much about their culture, and was a great oral historian. But this night he was not laughing. The lateness of the hour told me something was seriously wrong. No fool would be out in this weather at that hour just for a social call.

Tsumbu's expression and voice verified this, as did a quiet, shadowy figure behind him, just barely within the glow of my lantern. I strained to make out the figure of a tiny woman. Tsumbu noticed my startled reaction. He turned and called for her to come in. She had been standing there barefoot in the mud and downpour. I could feel her fear as she cautiously entered. A wrinkled old woman, I guessed her to be in her seventies or eighties. Aging can be deceptive in Africa, but I was sure she was of a veritable old age. Her bare feet were caked in mud to the ankles, and she wore traditional dress – a piece of cloth wrapped around her body and tucked with one end behind the other just above the breast. This was done somewhat like a woman back in the States would wear a bath towel after a shower. In the village this was the daily fashion as buttons and zippers had not yet found their way there. The elderly woman was soaked to the skin and the soggy cloth hugged her frail body.

I could sense her fear of me. I had lived there long enough to hear of the village's experiences with the French colonists and chicot, the whip! The only familiarity this woman had had with white men was with the French, whom she no doubt hated and feared. Stories of slave catchers were a large part of the oral history of the area; stories filled with extreme violence and abuse. I had often held back tears when they recounted their experiences. One story in particular told how a man was tied up and stuffed beneath the bed to listen as his wife was raped all night.

Standing there soaked, the old woman let Tsumbu do the talking and never once looked directly at me. The two night visitors were so frantic I couldn't even offer them towels to dry off, or even a hug of reassurance to the old, frightened woman.

"You have to take this woman's husband to the doctor, he's dying!" came Tsumbu's anxious request. I had heard old tales of the sick being carried on stretchers for days along paths through the jungle to see the "Great White Doctor" who I later learned was Dr. Albert Schweitzer. But the nearest doctor to our village was 50 kilometers distant – more than 35 miles! It was impossible for the woman to get her husband there in monsoon conditions on foot. But obviously my truck, the only one, offered her a new technology and hope for help.

I immediately agreed but did not voice the fears I had of the road conditions, dangers, and weather ahead. There are times of life and death where you just do what is necessary and reflect on the experience later. If you survive, you can then voice your surprise and thrill at what you've done. To go off the road in that weather with that jungle full of animals would be imminent jeopardy. Besides, there was no communication on the road; where we would be headed, no one was expecting us; no one would know how long we'd be gone; no one would be looking for us. No one else but similar fools would travel this night at all.

As the old woman heard Tsumbu's translation I could see a glow of gratitude and hope fill her face. Hope is a great thing; it seems to reinvigorate and make a person stand just a bit straighter. Tsumbu threw back, "We'll go get him!" as they hustled back into the storm.

I got dressed, and was drenched by the time I reached my truck 20 feet outside the door. Turning the truck around and facing back down the road to Koula Moutou and the hospital, I waited for the patient. In the downpour and with each flash of lightning, I could see a small group of people moving across the central area of the village toward me. As they arrived at the truck, I could make out a makeshift stretcher of two branches with a woven straw mat slung between, carrying the patient. I had not expected a stretcher; I thought the old woman and her husband would sit in the cab, out of the storm, but the old man would have to ride in the back on the cold, steel bed of the pick-up. Even on a sunny day, with good road conditions bouncing around on that steel truck bed would be misery, and that night the conditions were implosive. However, there was no other choice. My first thought was that the ride was going to kill the poor guy!

"That way? What's that way?" I yelled back, realizing that the way they wanted to go was south, up into the mountains. There was nothing up there but a few isolated villages, the jungle, and the Congo border. There would be no welcome ceremony there for an American. In fact, we volunteers had been told to stay away from the Congo, since it was a Cuban colony of sorts and they hated Americans. A person can disappear easily out there and no one would ever know how or why. I could end up the one in need of a doctor. But my passengers insisted they wanted to head south, away from the hospital I had thought was our destination. Since Gabonese would not go to the Congo, either, I reasoned we were going somewhere between our village and the border.

"But what doctor is up there?" I shouted.

"Our doctor," came the cryptic reply.

The collision of cultures had returned. I was intrigued, filled with adventure. This was fascinating to me as I realized we were going to see their beyem, or what people at home called a witch doctor. They also called their traditional doctors ngangas, or spiritual healers. Out of pure necessity, I had come into their confidence enough to be allowed to join in the trip. Perhaps now

I could really be thought as one of them, no longer considered a French Colonist.

The stretcher was hoisted into the back of the truck, then, to my irritation, the old woman was lifted up and sat down next to her husband on the truck bed. I thought she should be in the cab out of the storm. Was it her fear of white men that she could not be near me, I wondered? I quickly realized how egotistical this thought was. Next to her husband is where she wanted to be, and nothing was going to pull her away. It also came to my attention that these two lovers of many years had never been in a truck or any vehicle. This was their first ride. They couldn't know of the relative comforts of the cab, and both were terrified. It was only their desperation for the old man's health that surpassed their fear, or they would never have gotten into the truck at all.

With that thought of life and death, and the importance of the trip, I could not help feeling ashamed that I could not provide some kind of cover from the storm for them. One of the stretcher-bearers threw a straw sack and two chickens (feet tied with vines) into the truck and raced into the darkness for home. Tsumbu and I jumped into the cab. In 4-wheel drive low we started south into the mountains. I could see little ahead of us, my headlights reflected back off a wall of rain, as if in heavy fog. I knew what was out there, not just the dangerous mountain road, but also the animals. I could guess how happy they would be to see us fail. I had an eerie sense of driving through a zoo in total darkness knowing all the cages were open and all the animals were starving.

A mistake on the road could happen in the blink of an eye. If I allowed the tires to spin, they could easily dig into the mud and sink to the axles, and if I drove too fast, we'd loose all traction on the slippery mud and end our journey in the jungle. The trip would be over and what about the old people? How would we take care of them? We crept along and my whole body became tense from the concentration needed to stay on the road and moving fast enough to avoid getting stuck, but not one bit faster.

I was counting on Tsumbu not just as interpreter, but also as guide. I hoped he knew where we were and where we were headed. But at the time, I didn't fully realize he had walked these roads many times and could surely by instinct and experience, know exactly where we were. On foot he had passed here many times and knew every bend in the road. I should have asked before the trip and I would have been more confident that we would not pass by the village we were looking for. I pictured us looking down the machine gun barrels of the Congolese border patrols!

Tsumbu entertained me with his constant chatter and humor, a release of his own tension and a help to mine. He laughed in disbelief at the rain, the lightning, the slippery road, even at what would happen if the gorillas got hold of us. He was laughing the whole ride. I could not keep my concentration from drifting from the road to the two old people in the back, suffering the storm and the bruising ride. With a quick look through the back window, I could make out only the back of the old woman's head. She was tucked tight up against the rear of the cab, her head bent down, hiding from the rain. I could not see more, but knew her dying husband lay right there by her side. I imagined the touch and warmth of each other's body soothed that part of them where love exists, when everything else was misery. She would surely be cold and shivering from the loss of body heat given up to evaporate the constant flow of cool rain rinsing over her. I was impressed by her love for her husband, and knew she would put aside all misery to be there with this man she had certainly known since their youngest days in the village. My heart went out to them as they went through this experience of life together. Bringing my concentration back to the road, I thought the steering wheel I controlled was not just guiding us up the road; it was guiding us into a spectacular adventure. I was now in *National Geographic*, not just looking at the photos.

Finally, after hours, Tsumbu burst out, "Here, here it is! Stop!" The silhouettes of several huts were barely visible along the right side of the road. I had no idea what people were doing out this far, but then, I always wondered the same thing about people in the north woods of Wisconsin. Some people just prefer the peace and quiet away from the rest of human civilization. I stopped the truck and Tsumbu jumped out to disappear into the small array of huts. Returning after several minutes, he motioned us to follow him. Two men grabbed the stretcher, helped the old woman down, and led us to a simple stick walled hut with a grass roof. Inside we found only a fire pit in the middle and a few logs to sit on as we waited for the doctor. The atmosphere was eerie for me, but too fascinating to be frightening.

A chanting voice came gently from the darkness outside. As the chanting neared, Tsumbu told us, "It's him! He is coming!" I was shocked as the doctor entered the tent. No headdress! No beads dangling! No painted face! No ring in his nose! He was short and dressed as any other villager. Had we woken him in the middle of the night and upset him? Had he just not bothered with all that stuff this late at night? Or had *National Geographic* shown me a different culture? Though common in dress, I could feel an awe and reverence fill the hut. No one spoke, no one moved. I felt immediately honored to be a witness to this healing ceremony.

The doctor went to work. He knelt down near the fire, and pulled open a small animal hide sack that was tied around his waist. He cast what appeared to be small bones onto the ground in front of him. He stopped chanting, appeared to study the bones and seemed in deep thought. Then he rose, again began chanting, and slowly walked back into the night and the storm. The chanting drifted away, and then neared once more. The doctor reappeared to study the bones again. This studying and chanting off into the night was repeated three times. We remained fixed on the man and his activities. Finally, he spoke. In Tsumbu's language he was explaining what I guessed was his diagnosis. I was honored that I was allowed to be present, even if I couldn't understand what was being said. A few short sentences and it was over. The doctor was presented his fee - the two chickens, salt, and a piece of cloth. He gathered his payment, and with no ceremonial aplomb left our presence for good. Tsumbu and the old woman spoke softly and reverently, as though they were in any cathedral or place of reverence. The patient was then carried back to the truck, where his wife was lifted in to join him. We started back down the mountain.

The trip home was even more treacherous as the weight of the truck on the downhill slope pushed us faster and faster, endangering our traction. The trip that would have taken forty-five minutes in the dry season was now coming to an end after many hours. "So, what'd he say?" I finally asked Tsumbu. Thinking the answer would be an herbal remedy I was stunned to hear Tsumbu's response. "The old man is sick and dying because he has told a lie. Until he admits to the lie and tells the truth, he will not get well, and will die."

"That's it? That's all he said?" I blurted at Tsumbu. I was struggling to make sense of this. My culture gave me no background to fall back on for understanding such a diagnosis! But I realized history did. I was in a world of medicine before laboratories, blood tests, and X-rays, a place with no understanding of bacteria, viruses, and the microscopic world. External injuries are always visible and have a visible cause, but sickness with no physical injury had no explanation. Just as it might have been for us hundreds of years ago, this doctor searched for a cause, and a cure, if possible. I wondered how these traditional tribal healers had become so powerful and respected without any true understanding of causes and cures of illnesses. How could they never have been found out? Then it hit me. The diagnosis was fail proof. If the man died, he had not admitted to the lie. If he lived, he must have, in some way, corrected his dishonesty. The doctor couldn't lose; the cure was completely in the patient's hands. Of course, this diagnostic approach wouldn't persist at home. We'd be running for a second opinion faster than you can say MRI. But there in Lebangy these old folks believed fully in this practice, having never known any other.

Unfortunately, the old patient who returned to the village with us apparently never admitted to or corrected his lie. Several weeks later I was called on again to take him to the doctor. This time, we headed north to Koula Moutou, the French hospital and the white man's doctor. This time, the old couple had to endure another highly uncomfortable trip as the corrugated, steel truck bed was combined with a ruthlessly unforgiving dirt road. Shortly after arriving, the old man died. It must have taken great courage and desperation for the loving wife to overcome her fear of white men and seek out a medical doctor for her beloved husband. Her love and devotion remain strongly etched in my memory.

Of course, in the end, the man died at the hands of the white doctor. The woman and her family were left with the decision as to whether the white doctor's medicine was faulty and bad, and not to be trusted in the future, or to accept that they had simply brought the man to the French doctor too late for his medicine to help. I don't know what they decided. Maybe the man just lied, and that was that.

MURDEROUS POWER OF MATERIALISM

CHAPTER TWELVE

It was not just we in the Peace Corps service in Africa who faced collisions of culture. My encounters with Patrice brought that clearly home.

The demeaning rule of the French colonists had ended for most Central and West African nations in the early 1960's. The French had been brutal in their domination of the people and their plundering of natural resources. A general distrust and dislike of the French, while not often spoken, was in the air. It was this distrust that had to be overcome before we could experience the "real" Africa. The local people knew only their world; they were not familiar with maps, geography or politics. Their first experience of the outside world had brought them French white men. Consequently, they viewed all white men the same as the French. I felt I could understand their dislike, since I, too, had found the French arrogant. They seemed to continue to have an attitude of superiority over the Africans. It took quite a time, but eventually I earned the right to be recognized as different from the French, and this identification changed life for me in Africa.

However, the French rule was not entirely negative. Great improvements had been achieved. The educational system was one major example; high schools were built and staffed in most provincial capitals, and a university opened in the national capital. Those who qualified could emerge from the jungle villages to be formally introduced to the rest of the world. A good academic performance opened the door to the nation's new university, and for those few who performed especially well or were well connected, the doors to various universities of Europe were opened for the first time. These special few high achievers returned home to the reverence, respect, and envy of their fellow villagers. Many returned in the height of European fashion, their native dress discarded. It seemed as if even the new clothing heightened the awe given them; they had acquired a special power along with their new status in their old neighborhoods.

Patrice was one of these fortunate high achievers. When I first met him he was wearing his fine French clothes. He had studied engineering in France, and had been given the post of Head of Public Works for the town of Koula Moutou upon return from his studies. With electricity and indoor plumbing restricted to only a handful of new administrative buildings, Patrice's main and most important job was to keep open the road from the outside world. That dirt road was the only means of supply, and kept the city furnished with essentials. However, the task became formidable during monsoons. All Patrice's energy was spent on those roads. Almost humorous sometimes to view the eternal struggle between man and nature, there was no doubt, what with the monsoons a constant reminder, of who was going to win.

I found Patrice to be friendly and warm, never seeming arrogant, which he might have been considering his "high" position. He was a bit over 6 feet tall and slender in build. He wore a broad and genuine smile constantly; a smile that welcomed me when we came upon one another, but also infected me with a smile of my own and the anticipation of some easy, pleasurable chatting. We became good friends over time, and I would always stop for a few good laughs and moments of friendly conversation when I would find him hard at work on the dirt roads, supervising his limited machinery and his few men trying to accomplish his impossible task. Even working on those muddy roads in the monsoon rain, he wore his fine French business clothes, which always carried a spattering of mud. He was so proud of his achievements and position in the community. I was proud of him and happy for him, too, but it did create inner chuckles to picture our highway department in the U.S. supervised by men in fine Gucci business suits and ties. But such was the respect Patrice held in his community that his dress was accepted as fitting for his accomplishments.

Koula Moutou is laid out in an hourglass shape on the Ogouee River, which passes through the center of town at its narrows. The town is completely surrounded by dense, dangerous jungle. A single lane bridge connects the two sides; vehicles passing have to wait on one side for the opposite side to come across. One day during the dry season, I had come to Koula Moutou for supplies and found Patrice standing in the middle of the bridge, peering down into the river. I stopped as usual to greet him but there was no broad smile or warm greeting in return. Instead I met a face perspiring heavily and filled with anguish and distress. I asked immediately what was wrong. Wiping the sweat from his face, he replied in shaky, broken speech that his mom was missing. This statement startled me. I stopped the engine of my truck, jumped out and went to him. I followed his eyes over the railing down to the water. There, men were wading everywhere, searching the river. I asked Patrice what had happened. He was distraught as he explained that she had gone to the river to do laundry, and someone had found only the pile of clothes in the dirt on the riverbank, but not her. All I could do was stay there and try to console him while the men in the river below continued their search.

After some time I moved to the end of the bridge and climbed down to the river's edge. The frantic activity continued as the men scoured the river bottom. There was talk that the Panther D'eau, the water panther, might have snatched the missing woman from the shore. The Panther D'eau is akin to old wives tales, dragons, or the Loch Ness Monster, but still a possibility some locals considered. They didn't have a better answer: It was the dry season, no floods or rushing torrents, and it was hard to picture what problem occurred in the calm and gently flowing water.

Finally, I had to move on. The jungle is no place to be at night, and I needed to finish my day's task. I stopped for the latest update, but there was no news. Patrice's mother was still missing. I felt badly that I had to leave him alone on that bridge, but there was nothing I could do to help. I headed back into the jungle and home.

It was several days before I returned to Koula Moutou for diesel fuel. I stopped first to get news of Patrice and his mother. I was astounded to hear that they had found her in the river, and further, that Patrice was arrested for her murder! When they had pulled the body from the river, there were cuts over the body. A small piece of flesh had been cut from near each eye, each breast, and her female organs. The people identified this immediately as the signs of the village doctor.

As happens in the States, the police looked to the family first as suspects, and Patrice had confessed. He told them he had gone to the village doctor to explain his desire to be a wealthy man. He wanted all the material possessions he'd seen in France and wanted the village doctor to tell him what he needed to do to attain them. The village doctor told him to bring back these pieces of flesh from his mother's body, and all the wealth would be his! Patrice had done as told, and fulfilled the horrible request.

I was stupefied. How could any human being demand of another the killing of his own mother for riches? I knew that tribal doctoring was as old as their culture, but something was missing, didn't make sense. But I had been in Africa long enough by then to know that not all was as it appeared to my western thought process. Eventually, the explanation came to me, and was corroborated by others.

The village doctor had been as shocked as anyone that Patrice had actually fulfilled the required demands. He had meant to send Patrice the message that material things would not make him happy; had meant Patrice to realize the things that were most important were his family and their love. He had given Patrice the ultimate choice between his mother and material things. The village doctor assumed Patrice would understand there was no real choice, realizing that he was blessed with the wealth of his mother's presence.

Maybe the village doctor, too, had met a collision of cultures. For centuries the practices handed down were confined to the experiences from the jungle area within only a few kilometers. Now his people had experiences with far off cultures. They were bringing new unexpected challenges to his curative talents, much as a new virus challenges the modern world's medical minds. While the village doctor's trade was firmly planted in the past, some of his patients were stepping into the future.

Poor Patrice had definitely suffered his own collision of cultures, and the mix had taken him beyond reason. His home culture taught him the reverence for the village doctor and his advice. This same culture had greeted him on his return from France like a young god who was above all others. His university experience showed him lifestyles far beyond anything he had ever imagined. He must have been willing to accept such a life-shattering choice based on his new view of himself and his importance. Instead of using the advantage of his education to benefit his community, he became absorbed by self-fulfillment and greed.

Patrice was sent to the cold darkness of an African prison. These institutions are legendary for unrestrained torture, ending in death, and I am sure Patrice did not long survive his imprisonment. During the preceding months, as I thought back on Patrice working those muddy roads wearing his fine, mud spattered French clothes and broad, welcoming smile, the savage yet majestically beautiful jungle his backdrop, I felt such deep sadness for him and a certain sadness for the human race. It was curious and did not escape me that what I was running away from, Patrice would pay anything to have.

Patrice's story is one of the many lessons I learned in Africa that remind me to keep my desires in perspective, and appreciate the value of what is most dear in my life, my family and friends.

NATURE - THE GREAT PROFESSOR

CHAPTER THIRTEEN

It is hard for me to think of Africa without remembering the wildlife. From jungle to grassland to sub-Sahara, from army ants and termites to birds, behemoths, and of course, the vipers, there is no other display of diversity, color, shape, size, power, aggression, organization and pure jaw-dropping awe of spectacle like Africa. I was fascinated one day by giraffes, the next by elephants, the next by lions, and the next by snakes. The procession was endless, each presentation as majestic and beautiful as the one before. I would spend hours just watching a member of one species and never tire. Here, too, I would find a piece of the puzzle I was searching for to comfort my soul.

As a child back home I loved a day at the zoo and always looked forward to this with building excitement. I loved it all: Sam the gorilla, monkey island, the aviary, and the frightful, dark, clammy reptile house with deadly vipers, separated from me by only a pane of glass (which I was grateful for but couldn't help wondering what would happen if it all of a sudden broke). I believe our annual awe motivated my ma to give us children the visit to the zoo instead of just a park picnic or swimming at the county pool. On each trip, her ears were filled with rounds of, "Look at that Ma! Look over here, Ma! Wow, look at that!"

The zoo experience was alive and educational, with a view into other worlds of sea, sky, and far away lands that excited our young minds to great dreams of these animals and where they came from.

From those zoo trips I learned the importance of saving endangered species and educating the public on the need to protect and respect life. While I now appreciate that wondrous opportunity to see and learn, I think it is impossible to go through a zoo and not have the small voice somewhere deep inside whispering, "They should not be in cages; they should be free and running the plains, or flying the skies. They look so unhappy here." I had heard this voice on every visit, especially when viewing the biggest animals that had no freedom, no room to open up, let loose and just run. Maybe it was just some subconscious reminder of my ma's admonishments to "go to your room and wait for your father to get home." On these occasions I had also felt locked up, unhappy that I could not be out racing around with my buddies. But, in a sense, these animals had the better of it; they were not waiting for my dad to come home.

While in Africa, I would see the wishes of that voice come to fruition many times. I would be thrilled for these animals and know this was how life is supposed to be. To see a herd of giraffes in full stampede across a plain that goes horizon to horizon, kicking up dust trails, heads bobbing, legs flailing, is unforgettable. I was forced by existence to stop and take it all in. Like looking into the Grand Canyon for the first time, one can't just mumble "that's cool" and walk away. Something forces one to stop and just marvel, and for a short time there is nothing else in the world but that spectacle.

I saw many awesome sights while driving through the jungle. Once, just feet in front of the truck, a huge lowland gorilla crashed out of the jungle and landed on the road. Slamming on the brakes, I was shocked into sitting up straight, my eyes were blown wide open, and I gasped. For a moment there was no jungle, no road, no glass windshield and no truck, just that magnificent gorilla and me. I fixated on him, and could not believe the powerful, hairy figure hunched there before me. The legs, the arms with fists on the ground were extremely muscular, and the huge round head had fearless eyes that stared me down. Ferocious eyes that seemed to demand, "What are you looking at?" Only the screaming and pounding on the roof of the truck by the three villagers holding onto the roll bar brought me out of my stupor. They knew better, and were scaring the guy off. It worked. With knuckles pushing off the ground and a giant swoop, legs first, he crashed back into the jungle. I was as grateful for the visit as I was for the departure. Once again, as would happen so often, I would think how I was such a small part of something so much greater. How beautifully majestic is life in its diversity. I also realized how quickly my existence would cease if that gorilla had gotten hold of me. In but a moment, c'est rien! Nothing. Gone.

Some of the magic of the jungle was not only mysterious, but also deadly. Early one morning I heard screaming voices that came from just outside my house. Opening the back door I saw several neighbor boys wildly and frantically throwing clumps of dry hard clay. My eyes followed to their target. A shiny black, deadly viper was racing away from them. The seven-foot intruder made a fatal mistake and scrambled up a tree. I was impressed: these boys of nine or ten were hot after it, yelling "La Viper! La Viper!" and slamming more grapefruit sized chunks of hard clay at the intruder. As intended, the screams brought more neighbors, including two young mothers running to the scene. As they ran, they were bending on the way to grab clay and launching it treeward. With seven or eight neighbors now engaged and kicking up a small dust storm, the screaming continued loudly and wildly along with the onslaught. This was happening so rapidly that I just stood in the doorway, looking on in amazement. This was a deadly snake! But it had endangered the village, making these people just as deadly. This was not like throwing snowballs at squirrels, as I had done as a child. This,

I could feel in the air, had the endurance of a fight to the death. This snake could still be knocked from the tree alive, show its own survival instincts, become the attacker and kill someone. The fierce barrage with which these people were assaulting this snake was pure survival instinct. I knew it: I had seen it in war.

The screaming, the overwhelming volume of fire, the disregard for safety in assaulting a deadly foe, all these were the elements of combat. But these were young boys and young mothers, and all barefoot! More people arrived, screaming into action; some were carrying machetes. The snake, now about 15 feet up in the tree, was struck and blasted to the ground. The children did not run away, instead they charged, screaming harder and louder as the intensity of deadly danger increased. The snake was madly swirling around on the ground, confused and dazed by the heavy volume of clay filling the air around it. It was frantic to escape, but it couldn't. It was surrounded, trapped and overwhelmed by the assaulting villagers. There was a quick and perfectly aimed "swoosh" of a machete and it was finished.

As the dust settled, the combatants, breathing heavily, shifted their energy and went right to reliving the battle: "Where'd it come from?" "Who saw it first?" Others were telling of their own participation: "I hit it five times!" "Did you see how fast it went up that tree?" And of course the boys were arguing over who delivered the knock out punch: "I knocked it down!" "No, I did!" "You did not, I did!" "No you didn't, you can't even throw that high!" I was reminded of the same type of argument with my brothers and sisters.

The boys were burning off the nervous excitement of an adrenaline rush, which brought back memories of my own experience with pent up adrenaline after combat. While engaged in their reminiscences of the battle, an old man grabbed the carcass of the once deadly viper and raced off with what would now become a tasty meal for his family. He didn't seem to care about the bombardment of insults heaped on him for "stealing" the trophy that he had not helped to win. Calming down, the others slowly went back to reliving the event. The boys, pushing and shoving each other, returned to being boys.

I had been leaning on my doorway the whole time, watching this incredible scene take place. I was shocked at what I had just seen, realizing it qualified as a military maneuver! It was the textbook military response to an ambush, which was assault the enemy with overwhelming, deadly firepower. The screaming and absolute abandon of physical safety was a natural adrenaline component. But there was no military here! These were young boys and village women. I found myself preoccupied throughout that day and several more with what I had witnessed.

Another time news hit the village that one of the elderly women, while on her way back from her jungle garden, had been mauled and killed by a gorilla. Everyone was shocked and very sad. She was found dead and almost unrecognizable on the trail back to the village. She would have had no chance against such a powerful attacker. I pictured her horrified at the attack and how she must have suffered. Some of the hunters went out to investigate since it was unusual for a gorilla to attack, especially such a gentle old woman.

Lebangy is a small village where everyone is very close. The people rely on each other for survival and friendship. They are playmates as children, companions as young adults, they marry and raise families together, care for each other in sickness, and share their laughter and protect each other in the jungle that is a dichotomy of beauty and danger. The whole village mourned the loss of the elderly member deeply, and held a funeral around a large ceremonial fire. People came on foot from other villages to participate. During the ceremony, men and women took turns dancing in groups, slowly and somberly around the open fire, to the slow beat of drums. The fire also danced, throwing off shadows and dimly lighting the faces of the dancers, creating an eerie aura, and of course, in the backdrop, the front wall of the jungle flickered eerily in the flames. The smell and feel of the entire area changed as the wood burned in memorial service. Dancing and mourning went on late into the night as grieving was given its proper time to be expressed and shared. Later, the body was buried in a deep grave, deep enough to keep away animals.

It was curious to me that whenever I ventured into the jungle to get water, go to the river to bathe, or just for a walk, someone, by coincidence, was always going my way with "Hey, Myeke, where ya going? Really? Me too, I'll go with you!" It was the villagers' nature to know the surroundings, but they knew it was not mine. They respected the jungle and its deadly dangers, and worked with me until they were confident I could keep myself safe there. They were not afraid, just equal participants with the life. The jungle was no place for those who did not know it. Children were especially watched over, as we keep ours out of the streets at home. African mothers get just as frantic over a lost child as we do in America. Not because of cars, but because of the dangers of walking off, as all curious children do, into the jungle. I have always found it heartbreaking to watch a mother panicked over a missing child.

But what had happened in the incident of the elderly woman? I gathered with the men listening to the explanations of the hunters, and what I heard was heartrending and shocking. Those hunters who investigated were angry and showed it in their voices. A hunter, they said, had wounded a gorilla. Either he had not tracked it, as he should have, or could not find it as it ran off. The unsuspecting old woman, walking the path home, had come across not only the wounded gorilla, who was now dead, but also the gorilla's mate at her side. This second gorilla, thinking the woman responsible for the death of its mate, had viciously attacked and killed her. A gorilla does not just come up, put its massively powerful hands around your throat, and shake you like a rag doll. In its fury, it uses every muscle in the arsenal of its body; huge hands and fingernails powered by incredible arm strength, heaving chest and back muscles. The ferocious breathing and screams of a gorilla would be horrifying in its closeness. A gorilla has teeth that can rip through flesh, tearing it from the bones, hands that in one swipe could rip a face off leaving just a bloody skull. The deadly power is gruesome to consider. I could not let go of the image of the gorilla attacking the elderly woman.

My friend and mentor, Tsumbu, took me aside. "This woman was thought to be the killer of the gorilla even though she wasn't," he told me. "The gorilla's mate didn't know better." Then he very sternly told me, "If you surprise a gorilla in the jungle, you must not run! Never run! The gorilla will chase you down, and with its powerful fingers, rip the tendons from the back of your legs and kill you!" Tsumbu never spoke without animation; it is his unshakable habit learned long ago. I could find myself laughing at the most tragic message, not because of the contents, but at his physical and facial expressions. So it was this time. He continued, "If you do surprise a gorilla, you must stop, stand where you are, stand right where you are, and stare straight at the gorilla. Scream as loud as you can and keep screaming. With your hands and arms, wildly start clearing the ground in front of you." (Tsumbu was acting out each part.) " You are telling the gorilla, 'C'mon, I'm not afraid of you, see I am clearing a place right here for us to fight. C'mon lets fight!' You must keep this up and not stop until the gorilla leaves. If you stop, or run, he'll get you, he'll get you!"

I didn't know what to do first, laugh at Tsumbu's animated gesturing or absorb the critical message that might save my life. My thoughts were I'm dead: If I see a gorilla, I'm gone! I'm running! There is no way on the face of this earth that I was inviting a gorilla to a fight! I was certainly not going to build the arena where it would annihilate me! The mental image of this confrontation stayed with me a long time and reappeared each time I was alone in the jungle. I thought hard on what a nightmare that would be, what a way to go! But there was something in this event that I recognized but could not right then completely grasp.

I would witness many similarly brutal confrontations of survival in nature. All would have that same intensely vicious, insane madness. I watched two male lions in furious combat, fighting to the death. I heard the deep, bellowing roars of the assault and saw the air filling with dust as the two fearless warriors raced toward each other, muscles rippling in motion and colliding in fury. It was in this arena they had created right there on the grasslands of the Camerounian savannah that they would fight to the death. I could see the absolute disregard for anything but survival and the total concentration of all energy to that goal.

Another time an elephant attacked and killed two Frenchmen who either ignored, or didn't understand the elephant's three warnings to stay away from the herd it was protecting. I knew these warning signs, this language - they had been taught to me by the Africans. Once, when I was foolishly trying to get close for a good photo, I had quickly learned the importance of the warnings from an enormous bull elephant. Leader and protector of the herd, he will put himself between the herd and the danger. The first warning comes when he walks toward the intruder; waving his huge ears; a kindly voice saying, "Stay away!" For the second warning, he runs toward the intruder, ears waving, throws his trunk in the air and blasts out a trumpeting - a not so kind voice saying, "I ain't fooling, back off!" And for the third warning he races forward again, ears waving and dust kicking up, now trumpeting, "Get the hell outa here!"

Too preoccupied to apologize, I had retreated rapidly after the first warning and saw the second warning sent my way as I fled. But the elephant, understanding only its own language, gives just those three warnings and no more. If the warnings are not heeded, the elephant goes into defender mode and attacks. Then it is too late to negotiate; there are no peace talks, no truce, no apologizing with the promise never to do it again. There would be no again.

The two Frenchmen had not heeded the warnings and so were charged by tons of thundering gray anger, kicking up dust, roaring its attack. They must have been thrown into a state of fear that they did not know existed. Then, to seal their doom, they foolishly sought safety in a tree! What were they thinking? If inclined, an elephant can tear down trees just for something to do! To the elephant, they were still in his territory and a threat; a tree was hardly an obstacle for him. He pulverized the tree and stomped the Frenchmen into another life. The elephant, having spent its energy fending off the danger to his herd, then went casually back about his business of protecting the herd without any outward sign of regret.

It was the accumulation of these natural events that eventually opened my eyes to what I had recognized earlier but not fully understood. One of the effects that war had on me was the shame of having participated in the killing of other human beings for no reason other than my own survival; there was no other benefit. With my arrival in Vietnam the truth of that war and its absolute lack of purpose became a huge neon sign flashing in my mind. I would have been a fool not to notice that not once did I hear a thank you from a Vietnamese, military or civilian. Never did I witness an expression from those people that they were happy to see us and that they needed our help to survive. I could see no cause and find no reason to take human life there in that country. Nowhere, not even in the most remote corners of my soul, could I find evidence to honestly say, "Yes, killing these people has a reason; it is the right thing to do."

VENERABLE PYGMIES -
SO GRACIOUS, SO CONNECTED

CHAPTER FOURTEEN

Several years after arriving in Lebangy, no longer thought to be a white man or colonist - only Myeke, a member of the community - I was given a great honor that few have received. I was invited to meet the Pygmies in their beloved rain forest. Afraid of and lacking trust in the outside world, these people meet only whom they choose, or become shadows and disappear. If they don't want to be seen, they will not be. No one can track them. I thought how war had demolished my trust in the U.S. Government, and my fellow man. I understood the fears of these people whom I had only read about, yet with whom I felt a deep brotherhood. As they would retreat into the jungle to avoid humans, I too was there in the jungle, avoiding humans in my own way.

I had come along with the Gabonese government representative in charge of maintaining contact and correspondence with the Pygmies to monitor their conditions as these remarkable people were forced into closer contact with the outside world. Sadly, they were being forced into this by destruction of their habitat but more devastatingly, the destruction of their God, spirit world, and connection to their ancestors. We arrived on foot, deep in the darkness of the jungle; I in somewhat disbelief that the Pygmies were really going to step out of *National Geographic* and be real, and then there they were! I stood frozen as my mind raced over the vision before me. They were in every detail as the photos in that magazine had shown, except one. Yes, they were short, dark skinned, barefoot and traditionally dressed, but the bright, warm smiles that greeted me were not in the photos I had seen. I instantly felt welcomed, at ease and comfortable. I stood looking at a man, his wife, their children and several others of their group. They in turn, looked at me. I should have been listening to the interpreter but in my fascination I could not concentrate on words. How could this man who was at most 4 and one-half feet tall, with a wife who on tiptoes might have been as tall as her husband's shoulder, and these tiny little children all barefoot with simple waist clothing, live in this incredibly dangerous jungle? How could these people, who appeared so timid, docile and almost defenseless, be the same ones known to hunt and kill elephants with a simple machete? How remarkably they showed no fear, not of the jungle or us.

Then, finally listening to the interpreter, I learned that to remove them from here would destroy them; to these people the jungle is justifiably their god that fulfills every need of food, water, shelter, clothing, companionship, medicine and tools of survival. They had no other wants. In return, they were the caretakers of this jungle, their god. And before this god they were not afraid. I was stunned to think that this was one of the most plausible, realistic, applicable religions I had come across. I'll bet there were missionaries dying to get a crack at changing that, if they could find them. Luckily, from my viewpoint, they haven't been able to do so for millenniums. I was fascinated to notice that these people, living under the jungle canopy, would not have experienced celestial events, they would not have spent centuries studying the stars and deciphering "the meaning of it all." They simply loved their forest and life as it was, and had no complaints.

This culture and these people, according to anthropologists, date back seven thousand years. I imagined what it must be like to know your heritage for so long, to have walked the very same ground as ancestors did seven thousand years ago. What oral history they must have! I came from a country only several hundred years old and a family history on my father's side that went back only as far as my father, or twenty-nine years before my birth. I knew nothing of his parents, their country of birth or his relatives. I realized then I needed to know and understand better just who I was and where I was from. Maybe this would give me an understanding of the conditions over generations that resulted in my perception of the world. I would do this when I returned home – search for the important information hidden in that past.

After a wonderful visit, we said goodbye to these spectacular human beings whom I would never see again. I was sad about that, but grateful to have had the opportunity to meet them. I received a Pygmy's bow and quiver of arrows as a gift, a final remarkable detail of my visit with this ancient people. The bow was at most 18 inches long, the quiver simple tree bark, and the arrows about 12 inches long. There were no feathered quills, just a short, straight, sharpened stick. I had had toys larger than these as a child, but this form of weapon is all they had to use to hunt animals, defend their families, and live safely in the jungle.

I was most appreciative of the gifts of understanding that opened up inside me from my experience with these remarkable people. I came away more open to celebrating life, not complaining about it; determined to live every moment instead of being a victim; to love, respect, appreciate and take care of life as it appears in all its forms; to take control of and responsibility for my life; to stop relying on material possessions for happiness; to simply live life and not try to control it; and especially, to enjoy the simple things around me and stop thinking life to death. I felt I was learning not to be afraid of life, but to be afraid not to live it. And all of this from a people who have never seen, heard of, nor read a self-help book. A curious thought crossed my mind as I wondered, if they could read self-help books would they ask, "So when did you guys forget all this stuff?"

The rain forest, where the Pygmies live, must be one of the most complete science labs in the world, and science classes begin when nature decides. I was an enthusiastic student and anxious for each new lesson to arrive. So it was on a day that I was driving the road into Koula Moutou. It was the dry season and good sailing on the hard-packed clay road. With the usual suspects in the back of the truck and Tsumbu in the cab, I could make out what appeared to be a wide, straight swath of black painted across the road ahead. This looked out of place and even more so as we neared and I could make a gentle, black wavy motion to it. It was alive!

"Les fourmis! Les fourmis!" came the screams from the truck, to which I answered in excitement, "Well I'll be a son of a gun, army ants!" I stopped a few yards short of this 12-inch wide column, and we jumped to the ground and approached. Now one might think that the sight of creatures hundreds of times larger than themselves would have sent these ants panic stricken and fleeing in all directions, but they paid us no attention, maintained their formation, and went methodically toward their destination as if to say, "Sorry to interrupt you, we'll be out of your way in no time." The jungle was so dense I could not see how far their legions extended in either direction. I hunched down within inches to inspect closely, to look straight down on this life in motion. I could see only tightly packed individuals all so strongly entwined that no ground was visible between them. Had these been humans, they'd be tripping all over each other, but these six legged guys had marching down and worked well together. I looked on in fascination at the much larger ants with huge pincer like crab claws who, acting like guards, flanked both sides of the column and kept the others in formation. There had to be communication going on between them; whatever it was I was not included and heard nothing. Yet, for so many,

many thousands upon thousands of individuals to be as well organized as the Roman Legions was impressive, and I felt an awareness that nature was laughing at my ignorance.

Yes, I had heard stories that these intrepid hunters had carried off children, but that had happened in many other fairy tales, too. After a few minutes of captivation it occurred to me that the other guys were also watching; they were not frantically stomping on the ants or wanting to destroy them. They explained that these ants "were good and ate the bad stuff." I was told that when these ants come to the village, everyone watches where the ants go, gets everything of importance out of their way, and lets them eat up the bugs, scorpions, even snakes, in a kind of good house cleaning. These people knew so well how to live as a part of nature, and that all of life had a purpose. I could not help but think that by now, at home, there would have been a fleet of exterminators on the way to dump heaps of chemicals on this wonderful display of nature. I did not know how long the column would take to cross and the guys with me could not say either, but I knew one thing for certain, I was not driving over them!

We returned to the village to wait a few hours. I would never see army ants or Pygmies again, but was thankful for that one meeting with each of them, teaching me an even deeper respect for all living things. I have often fallen to sleep, thinking of them, now as a real experience for me, not a dream from a magazine. And I always hope they are happy out there in their beloved jungle, because I am well aware that life has its paradoxes.

Within kilometers of where I had met the humble Pygmies, caretakers of the rain forest, I happened to meet Jacque, a man who had other ideas for that place. He had come from France and set up shop along the dirt road leaving Alembe for Lastoursville. With modern technology in the way of heavy earth moving equipment, he had only one purpose, which was to clear the rain forest and expose the huge Okoume hardwood trees for cutting and loading onto a procession of lumber trucks for transport elsewhere. Of course, this was not a surgical procedure that avoided destruction of other life and growth; it was pure destruction of everything in his way. I had to look at him and mutter to myself, "Yep, I have just witnessed a mindless human being; they really do exist!"

Jacque had come from his French homeland with one thought, to make himself rich as quickly as possible, and then return home to live in luxury. This I know because he told me. I wondered how many people had used the bounty of Africa for this goal, leaving their spoils behind? Jacque had also been well equipped to rough it out in the wilds. With a gasoline generator he was furnished with refrigerator, freezer, electric lights and regular provisions of food and household goods. Living alone in a well built, western style home, he lacked little and seemed happily isolated from any pesky neighbors. When not deforesting the earth and dreaming of wealth and how great that life would be, he had few other interests. Bathing or rubbing shoulders with a bar of soap was obviously not high on the list, and apparently never had been.

Jacque was a short, stocky man, given to wearing button down shirts worn unbuttoned over an undershirt whose cotton fibers had long ago succumbed to fatigue, and whose size had shrunk to expose his big, sweaty stomach that hung easily over his low riding waist band. A day's work would leave a film of dirt-crusted sweat across his clothes and body. Of course, dirt and sweat did not bother him for it was whiskey that the end of his day required. The only dust he washed away was in his throat. Withdrawing from his stash a bottle of Johnny Walker Red, he would throw away the cap, knowing he would not be need of it again.

And so I learned of this man (one of many I am sure) whose sole purpose was to destroy the cathedral home of the most honorable people I had ever met. Today, as the intensity of rain forest destruction continues, I read many accounts of rampaging elephants furious at the loss of their habitat, and I listen to those concerned with the elephants' plight. But I question if people are just as aware that destroying the rain forest causes heartbreaking desecration of the Pygmies' sacred way of life, which is akin to the impertinence toward the Sioux Nation's spiritual beliefs when whites desecrated their hallowed Paha Sapa – the Black Hills - in South Dakota; not to mention other atrocities the U.S. Government has inflicted on them and other American Indians under the greed disguised as "Manifest Destiny."

I do know that some of the Pygmies are now turning up in the African cities as street beggars. I wonder if Jacque, surrounded by his self-serving, greed-gotten luxury in Paris, ever thinks of this.

CRITICAL REFLECTIONS ON WAR

CHAPTER FIFTEEN

I have talked to many combat veterans of World War II, looking to them for something but I was not sure what that "something" was. To a man, each said one of two things: "We had to stop Hitler," or, "We had to stop the Japanese." After hearing this repeated over and over, the answer came to me. This was the soulful balancing act for these veterans. This was the "something" they had in their souls to justify the horrible experiences of war. They had been involved in taking human lives, but could always fall back on a valid reason to maintain some balance in their souls. They were defending a true threat to their nation, to their families, and they held a justification for war: survival. Through them I saw why shame, darkness, and torment had taken over my soul: I had no balancing act. I could search the depths of my soul and find no reason, no acceptable logic that I could force myself to believe, or that could justify my participation in taking human lives. I could not fool myself and divine some reasoning for this, other than my own survival.

I frequently refer to my soul: This is where the battle resides for me, where the damage was done and where I have focused my repair work. I can see no value in holding on to the anger and knowledge of so many years ago. Being frozen in that time and those horrendous experiences has become more frightening than the causes themselves. I think of my soul as the engine in a car. If that engine stops running, it would make no sense to wash and wax the car so that it looks good for the neighbors. Nor would it make sense for me to sit in the house and hope that someone would magically show up to fix it. Little benefit could come from filling myself with rage, blaming the auto industry, the salesman who sold it to me, or searching the whole world for a place to lay blame. I have to open the hood, find the problem and fix it. It's the same with my soul. By fixing my life, my soul, I can get back on the road heading to where I want to be. It is my soul; it belongs to no one else and it is my responsibility to care for it. To pass time concerned with what the external world thinks of me is ridiculous and is not where the problem or the answer exists. To create the image of the unaffected veteran for society's sake is foolish thinking. To place blame on the military, the government, the protestors, is a pathetic avoidance of the truth. I have to open the hood of my soul, look inside, find and fix the problem, every problem.

I could peer into what I had thought was that darkness in my soul and confront the ugly human hiding there. One aspect of trauma is the fear that what I had experienced in war was too complicated, too overwhelming to face. I was afraid that I could not confront the issues and resolve them; that there would be no answers. And that those issues must be left behind the facade I had created. But this was exactly the thinking that would doom me to a life locked in those same unresolved issues, an eternal circle of my own misery.

I remembered at war how the most frightening thought was of walking into an ambush. Training had told us that you must attack the ambush with overpowering, suppressive firepower. The idea of running into a wall of machine gun fire and grenades seemed at first a form of insanity and sure death. But when thought out, it is the right thing to do, the only thing to do. If you are running away, the enemy has only to shoot you freely as you flee. If you

attack with as much fire power as you can, the enemy will have
to take cover to protect himself, and then cannot continue firing
at you. It is a frightening concept, but true.

But is this idea an intellectual decision to attack or is it survival?
I saw the answer all around me in Africa. Something was in the
boys and women who killed the snake in the tree; the courageous
faces of the Pygmies in the jungle; the men who knew how to
fight off a gorilla; the gorilla who killed the old woman; the two
lions fighting to the death; the elephant protecting his herd; and
it was in the guys in my truck who scared the gorilla off the
road. This something was survival. I realized that survival was
everywhere in life. It can no more be removed from a person or
animal than the need for water or food. One needs the survival
instinct to exist. In none of the above mentioned episodes were
there rules of engagement, Geneva conventions, truces, Marquess
of Queensbury rules, rules of war, a concept of fighting clean,
or conventional warfare. There was no shame, no guilt. It was
survival: kill or be killed. Nothing more, nothing less.

When I realized what I had seen in Africa, and thought of my
self-hatred, shame, and guilt for having participated in a war
without a cause, and how I had painted my own soul dark for
having done so, I saw something different. When we were in
firefights, I was not fighting to defend a homeland, trying to take
out an evil dictator, or trying to liberate a people; it was the same
survival "something" I saw in Africa. It was those exact times and
places, those conditions right then, as well as now, that required
the trait of survival to be employed. As there was no shame in
any of the instances I had witnessed in Africa, there was no need
nor reason for me to have shame. To have the characteristics of
my species is no shame, it is reality, and not to have it would
leave me lacking in being a complete human being. Those who
have never experienced the need to survive, do not understand
who they truly are.

Now I saw that it was I who had called my soul dark, not
others. No one, no country could make my soul dark without

my permission. If it was a result of social upbringing, religious beliefs, intellectual teachings, so it was. Was I incorrect to have believed some things as I grew up? No, those beliefs fit my reality then, but my reality changed and so must my thinking. I now realized that I am normal to have the instinct to survive and the responsibility to use it properly. I could take the darkness out of my soul. People can intellectualize that we are "better than that" all they want, but when the need to survive presents itself, intellectualizing goes out the window. Any mother can tell you this. If we were better than that, we would not be sending people off to war. To be honest about the instinct to survive has nothing to do with being "better than that," it is the reality of the existence of this trait.

It also became clear to me there in the African jungle that when in survival mode, one cannot totally rely on religion or social upbringing, but rather pure animal reaction. It would seem much more realistic for our leaders to use religious and social beliefs in making the decision to go to war. But then having made the decision, understand that those who are sent off to war will have no choice but to rely on the survival mode, and not their religious beliefs or social learning. I disagree with those who say that animals have instincts but humans have intelligence and no instinct. Living in a textbook can be dangerous. Many times I have witnessed the survival instinct in humans and animals, and they always appeared the same.

Now, leave the African jungle and step back to that other mountain jungle with me. We infantry soldiers were "humping" in the jungles of the central highland of Vietnam, with the weight of rucksacks straining our backs, and suffering the tropical heat. We were on hyper-alert for any movement, smell, or noise. Communication was by hand signals or whispers as no noise would be tolerated. There was no rattling of equipment and great care in placing each step to avoid the embarrassment of being the idiot who carelessly gave up our position to the other team. Under these strains of discipline, we were descending one hill, crossing a short valley, and climbing back up the hill on the other side. There were four of us crossing the valley at a time, maintaining safe distance from each other.

I was crossing the valley with a man named Tom in front of me when an explosion of movement on our left raced toward us in the tall grass. The movement was so fast that by the time we (who were vigilantly on guard for this) could turn to the left to face the danger, it had already passed between us, and was gone into the tall grass on our right. Our hearts were pounding loud enough to give up our position when we realized the attacker was a frightened dog deer! That tiny terrified deer had just about caused two of the world's best-armed and trained infantry soldiers to soil themselves, with nerves stretched taut to their limit. Tom raised his M-16 above his head with both hands and then slammed it to the ground as he screamed at the top of his lungs, "I quit!" I also snapped and fell into unrestrained laughter. With lives and our position in the jungle compromised, we had no choice but to laugh at the insanity or be consumed by it. Tom had been startled beyond his limits and the energy had to go somewhere! So, it went into laughter. But this was also the same energy that would be released in actual combat. All things considered, I'd rather laugh! The point here being we were at war, it was too late to rationalize, and it was time to survive; every cell in our bodies was focused on this. But, thank goodness, we did not alert the other team to our whereabouts.

In my uncontrolled laughter, I blurted out to Tom, "So, what're you gonna do, catch a bus home?" The reality of our circumstances hit quickly, control was regained, and we were restored to intense hyper-attention to survival. The release of laughter helped tremendously.

I finally came to the realization that this intellectualizing and ceremonializing of war was purely foolish, if not lunacy. Writers of history books might paint war gloriously, I found it insanity. I accept that I have this instinct to survive, that I used it, that it is normal at this time in the progress of the human race to possess it, and it is not darkness. Equally important, I realize that in my thinking, nothing can be as important as knowing the truth of my soul. I had spent years avoiding what lay inside there, and it now makes sense to want to understand every strand of truth in there. I had been unable to sleep well for years, and realized that if I wanted to sleep in peace, I could not fool myself with phony interpretations of what I found inside my soul.

Again it became the highest importance to see, hear, and know the truth about myself. What the world outside my soul believed had little value for me: it was what I felt the world outside my soul thought that had devastated it in the first place. I realized that if I approached my soul with honesty, I would not be able to focus blame anywhere before looking toward myself. I realized that I had had the choice not to go to war. That yes, I could have chosen prison, run and hidden from war, left the country, or gone to college. Nevertheless, I had chosen to go to war and I had chosen not to study the war before going. But I had also listened to other voices. I had believed teachings of honor, country, and duty. I had listened to the "story of honor" that called me to avoid embarrassing my family. I had believed in the leaders of the country, my religion, the military, and my countrymen. I had honored those beliefs, but when I realized how shatteringly those beliefs had failed me, it was still my responsibility to take the new information and adjust my reality.

But this was not easy when all of the beliefs that formed my reality collapsed cataclysmically at the same time. Now I needed to rebuild my soul by listening to my own truth. But this truth would have to be so painstakingly clear that when I lay down to sleep at night, I would know that the one person I could not fool was in charge. I had to accept that if I listened to myself honestly and without fear, I would find comfort and peace, not in the outside world but inside. I could no longer lie to myself. I would have to know the truth inside me and recognize that no other truth could be given more importance.

Just as I have the instinct for survival, so does the human

race. The reality that humans have been going to war since the beginning of time is proof that war was not developed the day I was born simply to punish me. I had to accept intellectually there is a view of human life without war, and that to some the thought of war is repulsive. To have all humans think this way is certainly a great goal, but reality has shown that the human race has never come close to this goal. I do appreciate and respect peace demonstrators who push for the idea of life without war, but until this comes to fruition, we all will have to deal candidly with the existence of war and survival in the human race.

Mark Twain's "The War Prayer" shows one man's honest look at the reality of war: A stranger had entered a church where the pastor was leading the congregation in a prayer for their young soldiers. The burden of its supplication was that an ever-merciful and benign Father of us all would watch over our noble young soldiers and aid, comfort and encourage them in their patriotic work. Bless them, shield them in the day of battle and the hour of peril, bear them in His mighty hand, make them strong and confident, invincible in the bloody onset; help them to crush the foe, grant to them and to their flag and country imperishable honor and glory.

An angry old man rises and, in short, explains that they have made two prayers, one uttered, the other not, and both have reached Him who heareth all supplications, the spoken and the unspoken. He exhorts them to be aware that it is like many of the prayers of men, in that it asks for more than the requester is aware of. He explains that in their prayer for victory they have also prayed for unmentioned results which cannot help but follow victory. The old messenger of God then puts into words the unspoken part of the prayer.

THE WAR PRAYER

"*O Lord our Father, our young patriots, idols of our hearts, go forth to battle - be Thou near them! With them, in spirit, we also go forth from the sweet peace of our beloved fireplaces to smite the foe. O Lord our God, help us to tear their soldiers to bloody shreds with our shells; help us to cover their smiling fields with the pale forms of their patriot dead; help us to drown the thunder of the guns with the shrieks of their wounded, writhing in pain; help us lay waste their humble homes with a hurricane of fire; help us to wring the hearts of their unoffending widows with unavailing grief; help us to turn them out roofless with their little children to wander unfriended the wastes of their desolated land in rags and hunger and thirst, sports of the flames of summer and the icy winds of winter, broken in spirit, worn with travail, imploring Thee for the refuge of the grave and denied it - for our sakes who adore Thee, Lord, blast their hopes, blight their lives, protract their bitter pilgrimage, make heavy their steps, water their way with their tears, stain the white snow with the blood of their wounded feet! We ask it, in the spirit of love, of Him Who is the Source of Love, and Who is the ever-faithful refuge and friend of all that are sore beset and seek His aid with humble and contrite hearts. Amen.*"

Had I been present in that congregation, I would have been enlightened by this truth. More importantly, after hearing this, I would have questioned then, as I do now, why go to war without a substantial reason for protecting your own?

LIVING ON NATURE'S CLOCK

CHAPTER SIXTEEN

Life in the village drifted along slowly and peacefully. With no clocks to haunt me, life happened as it happened, not by some frantic schedule. No one was ever in a desperate hurry to get somewhere; a habit I acquired and enjoyed. Clock time was for other places, not here. Morning, afternoon, evening, day and night were time to these people. The old adage "time is money" made no sense as currency was rarely used. The jungle was the provider of their currency; it was the "central mint." The jungle provided a food supply, water, building materials, medicinal barks and herbs, items for barter and more.

Outside of wanting to be an explorer or photographer for *National Geographic,* I had often thought of becoming a craftsman. I have always enjoyed and respected the trades and the people in them. I find pleasure in watching a true crafts-person who knows how to use tools. The great benefits – the pride put into the work, each tool performing its particular task, and assembling a finished masterpiece of which to be proud. The love of teaching and the pleasure derived from doing so is also special. I enjoy teaching or, as said in the trades, transferring skills, so I was delighted to have the opportunity of transferring to four men the skills of masonry, cement finishing and carpentry, as we set out to build a small three-room school.

It is important for me to remain focused on those experiences I consider to have given me insight into Post Traumatic Stress. I will mention that we did work hard on the school and three baked, earthen brick teachers' houses. Except for cement and nails shipped out from the capital, all materials were found locally. Sand and gravel were taken by shovel from the river and screened for size. Lumber was rough sawn by hand from trees taken out of the jungle. Simple tools, handsaws, hammers, framing squares and an old fashion water level - whose use can be traced back at least as far as the construction of the pyramids – were our tools. In going there to teach, I was amazed how much I learned! I think often that the people of Lebangy taught me much, much more than I left behind.

I will admit to a great sense of pride when the school opened, not so much for the actual construction but the unanticipated enthusiasm of the children. Bare feet and tattered clothes could not hide the excitement and pride that glowed from them as they went off to school. Each student carried a small 6 by 8 inch paper-covered, lined notebook, a possession that each seemed to treasure immeasurably. I imagined each child clutched his or her notebook when going off to sleep, as I had done with special joys of my childhood. How much more treasured this notebook would become with each new day's entry using their newly acquired ability to write! The world outside their own began to open up to them. I could see how the body expressed the joyful soul in these kids as they walked with heads held high and backs straight. They seemed to walk and run with a gentle, light ease of motion, the faces flooded with smiles and eyes that twinkled with the delight of life. Spoken words were not needed to understand the condition of their spirits; they spoke in so many other ways.

I remembered my body showing the opposite back in the jungles of Vietnam as I stood over dead bodies. When I felt "something" leave me as my head and shoulders slumped forward, my steps became heavy and plodding, and my eyes became frozen orbs that were haunting, cold and lifeless - a reflection of the condition of my exhausted spirit. But to witness these children experiencing such joy at something I had helped to provide made me stand straighter, my eyes sparkled, and my soul smiled warmly. I had seen the hideous side of humans as well as the beauty; there was no doubt that making the world better at any level was the balancing act my life required after war.

I laughed the first time I took the men who worked with me out into the jungle to search for wood to be used in construction. We split up and were to meet back on the road after a while. In my search, I saw trees, endless trees. I was searching for good, tall, straight lumber to be sawn by hand for construction lumber. Meeting back on the road, the other guys showed up, but looking like they had just come from a shopping center. They had arms full of all sorts of "finds."

"Whatcha got there?" I had to know! With the excitement of people returning from Christmas shopping, they had to show off each item.

"This (a root) is spice for my wife's cooking!" "This (a vine) is for making a mat, and repairing my wife's work basket!" "This (a piece of bark) is medicine; it's good for headaches!" "These (a bunch of leaves) boiled, are good for the stomach!" "These (large leaf folded up) are slugs; they are really delicious!" (Unfolds leaf to show off a mass of lively, fat, wiggling caterpillars.) The man then took one vigorous victim in his fingertips, popped it in his mouth, chewed dramatically and "mmmed." While he was busy "mmming," I gently shook my head back and forth. "No, I don't want to try one!" My expression let him know he had me on shaky ground and this pleased him to childish laughter. Holding a second wiggly "treat" in my face, he took humorous pleasure in chiding me. "C'mon, try one, just one, they're delicious!" When younger, I probably received the same wide-eyed pleasure while chasing and tormenting my sisters with worms, but I had lost my appetite for anything to do with this type of hors d'oeuvres long ago. My heckler could not help tilting his head back and moaning with theatrical ecstasy as he slid the second squirming treat down his throat.

Although this bordered on disgusting to me, to him, these were as wonderful as a box of fine chocolates. I considered the possibility of my taking these chubby grubs back to the finest restaurants in America, sautéing them in butter, adding just a dash of exotic spices, and offering this delicacy to the refined palate, restricting it by price and position on the menu just above escargot. I'd become rich and the consumers would be delighted by the stature this delicacy would lift them to! I could do nothing but laugh, not at the men, not at myself, but at some phenomenon in life that reminds me over and over that I don't know everything, that life is wonderfully diverse and has different values to different folks.

In the jungle, I had seen trees, nothing but trees. I would have to look more closely next time I thought, so that I, too, could find these treasures. Well, maybe not.

We returned to the village, the men pleased with teasing me about their delicacy. I knew there had been a time not too long ago that I would have needed to prove my masculinity by taking one of those fat, wiggling creatures, stuffing it in my mouth, and grinning with as much pleasure as I could invoke, no matter how repulsive in taste or texture. But war had given me a different insight into the idea of masculinity, and it wasn't about eating fat, juicy insects to impress others. Why had the men not found any lumber for construction? I didn't ask and they didn't tell; why spoil a good day's shopping for them? Besides, there would be time again tomorrow.

Being an American, I had arrived in Lebangy prepared to battle nature with black, mid-calf, heavy leather snake boots, denim pants and heavy, long sleeve shirts to fight off the hoards of mosquitoes and tsetse flies that I knew were thirsting for an international blood donor. I had believed that my biggest concern would be the dangers of the deadly animals, and had pictured myself desperately fleeing from the attack of the dreaded Gaboon Viper and its 2-inch venom filled fangs, or fleeing in wild panic from the deadly assaults of lions, gorillas, wild buffaloes and rampaging elephants. I could see myself in the coil of a boa constrictor that had its own opinion of my waist size and its desire to reduce it. I had thought these animals would be everywhere stalking humans. How wrong I was! Although I saw many, not one viper took a chance at those boots, and although we ate them, never did a boa constrictor take an interest in me. The big animals were not everywhere, stalking, hiding behind trees and houses, or chasing me around the jungle or village. I guess the animals have calmed down since Tarzan movies, or maybe that was all just for the cameras and a bit of drama, since all those were filmed in New York's Central Park.

An animal killed only one villager during the entire time I was there: the woman killed by the gorilla. And although the snakes were everywhere, not one of the barefoot villagers was ever bitten. The animals are not sinister creatures wandering the jungle, killing just for something to do. Snakes did come into the village but had a poor record of success against their formidable, barefooted foes. In the jungle snakes and animals avoided humans if warned of their arrival, and this is exactly what the villagers did by communicating with them. They made noise by singing, talking, and making sure to shake branches as they moved through the jungle. Some parents protected their children with "early warning signs" such as small rattles made of dry gourds tied on a small piece of vine, or small chains of bells worn around the ankle. Always, the villagers announced their presence to the life in the jungle as they approached.

But there was another deadly world in the jungle that I named the little world. It was the world of mosquitoes, tsetse flies, unseen viruses, and bacteria that wreaked the most havoc in this country, and gave me another great lesson and piece of the gigantic world puzzle. I am not a doctor or medically trained, so what I recount here is what I witnessed and not intended as medical fact, but it is close. Horrible diseases ravage Africa. The hardly visible life disclosed the real suffering for these people, and showed up in malaria, dysentery, diarrhea, filariasis, schistosomiasis, dengue fever, sleeping sickness, and elephantiasis, which caused horrible oozing, infected sores on their leg.

It seemed nature was bent on a vengeful assault on people who did not deserve it. Especially hit hard were the children, infants and young pregnant women. I had to constantly remind myself that these people lived in a world before the microscope, before knowledge that some deadly things exist that cannot be seen. The people had no medical or scientific understanding of why these diseases occurred. I had to imagine that over the centuries they must have, in desperation, sought reasons and cures in what we would call quackery and witch doctoring, sorcery, omens, and superstitions. Some didn't work, but others did. Many of our modern medicines are derived from plants and other sources that were first used by indigenous people. What was missing was the underlying understanding of disease – only discovered in the West. We aren't really all that far ahead, after all.

My heart went out to all of those over the centuries who as responsible, frustrated leaders had seen their people get sick and die with no outward signs, no wounds. With no answers, they could only helplessly stand by and watch. Physical wounds could be explained; disease could not. I heard of and saw applications of "cures" that were shocking: I saw people with very sharp knives cutting slits in the skin of the forehead, chest, and arms, to get the "bad blood" out that was causing them pain. I never said anything; it was not my place to do so, but I also know that blood letting killed many people in Europe and America not that long ago. Western medicine considered Mercury a cure for Syphilis into the 1900's There were herbal remedies and treatments and some were effective, but only for adults. Small, sick children and babies wanted nothing to do with water or these medicinal treatments; they would not take them. Even the village doctors had no remedies.

I have wondered what would happen if I transported one of these viruses home and it thrived with no known cure? Ebola was later found right there in the area where I had lived. How fast would humans learn the foolishness of man-made war in the face of a true adversary?

I was once treated for a form of severe, dysentery by my neighbor, a wonderful woman, who was the mother of eight children. She was a great mom and loved the job. In raising her children, she became familiar with the traits of each child. If an eyelash fell from one child, she'd notice something was amiss. She'd inspect that child from end to end and from all directions hunting for the "thing" that was not right. With her thumb, she would drag a lower eyelid down to the top of the child's cheek, and peer into his eye; the palm of her hand would check first the forehead, then the cheeks for fever. This was followed by a prepared list of questions: "Do you feel sick?" "Where does it hurt?" And on and on. Mothers have this intuition and can't be fooled. My own mother had this ability; she saw "it" when something was different. When she was new to motherhood, we noticed the attention given us when my mom detected an infirmity; we also saw in this a loophole good for a free pass to avoid school or a task. With a well timed, "Mom, I don't feel good," we would get her attention. After inspection and finding no real symptoms, but being a young mom new to the business, she would give us sympathy and pampering. However, it did not take long for her to accumulate experience. She learned to sniff out a phony whine and medicate the afflicted with a stern, "get dressed, you're going to school!" The scowl on her face and the fists ground into her hips reinforced the diagnosis. There would be no cooing sympathy, hot soup, couch, blanket, or cartoons that day.

So it was with my neighbor in Lebangy. She had come to watch over me as one of her own little "charges." When I received the gift of dysentery - a very painful, disabling disease - it was not diagnosed by lab tests in a hospital, but by the trained eye of a mother who saw me springing from my house and racing through the dirt to the outhouse. Several of these round trips, closely spaced in time, and she had her own diagnosis. And so did the entire village!

When a mother is at the job of nursing her sick, she is single minded. She cares little for any humiliation that accompanies her treatment. If she catches you in your underwear or other embarrassment, she doesn't much care about it. She is there to administer her remedy, and administer it she will!

I was seated in a chair bent over from the agony attacking my stomach and the burning pains and inflammation of evacuation elsewhere, when my neighbor burst through my back door. "Drink!" she commanded me, putting an earthen bowl of hideous, thick, green slime to my face. "Drink!" She gave me no time for any reaction. "Open!" With one hand on my forehead, she pushed my head back, and down my throat slid the hot, putrid ooze. With the confidence of a loving mother who knows she has done the right thing, no matter how painful, she said, "there!" and left.

In the short time it took for her medicine to course through my system, all symptoms disappeared. It was that quick! And oh, how very grateful I was! She later laughingly explained she had given me a leaf from the jungle she had boiled and pounded into a semi-liquid. I have no idea what leaf it was, but I saw her obvious satisfaction with her success.

PART THREE
ANOTHER KIND OF WAR:
DEATH, DISEASE, DYING

"Who can describe the injustice and cruelties that in the course of centuries they [the colored peoples] have suffered at the hands of Europeans? If a record could be compiled of all that has happened between the white and the colored races, it would make a book containing numbers of pages which the reader would have to turn over unread because their contents would be too horrible."

- Dr. Albert Schweitzer, *On the Edge of the Primeval Forest*

Dr. Albert Schweitzer went to Africa to - in a small way—make up for the historic guilt of European colonizers. And though I would arrive in Gabon more than half a century after this profound sense of reparation brought Dr. Schweitzer there, I would witness by lingering attitude and oral history the barbaric nature by which these people were devastated in spirit, resources and economy. This hideous assumption by the colonists that their apparent superiority of morals and values legitimized the imposition of their life style was simply a cover for the force used to rape the people for pleasure, disregard their culture and its importance to their very existence, and acquire all that the environment could be forced to surrender for their uncontrollable greed.

TIMES OF TRUE SUFFERING

CHAPTER SEVENTEEN

I found no "bug juice" in Africa to counter the ruthless appetite of mosquitoes for our blood. We slept under mosquito nets, but we could not live there. People in the village used a shredded bark that did not burn but smoldered in the fire. It was somewhat effective if you sat just next to the fire pit, didn't move around and didn't mind a dose of asphyxiation. I don't know who figured it out and little did I care, but a light coat of diesel fuel applied like a repellent was a miracle discovery. For the misery it saved us, it was a discovery more important than electricity. Not only mosquitoes, but also bugs did not approach, nor did the neighbors. But the fuel had to be diesel, not kerosene or gasoline, for these will burn the skin and more dangerously, explode! Washed in diesel fuel, I would laugh wondering if the prefect in Koula Moutou would still suggest I find a woman? And if I did find a woman who didn't mind a man who wore diesel fuel for cologne, I know we would have little in common. Regardless, the diesel fuel worked and I used it with the pleasure of Old Spice!

In spite of the shredded bark, diesel fuel and mosquito nets, malaria is still one of the most common deadly diseases in Africa. It is a deadly, seven-to-ten day battle with raging fever, headache, and total body aches during the day, and incredibly profuse sweating and uncontrollable cold shivering at night. During the time of high fever, a person feels close to a coma, has no energy, can't move and doesn't want to. It is a battle just to survive.

I would suffer three bouts of malaria, two overseas and one in Wisconsin. The first episode hit me when I was fortunate enough to be out of the bush and near a hospital. My body temperature went so high I was put on a mattress of freezing alcohol. If there is such a thing as good news coming out of malaria, I received it, for I had vivax malaria and not the more deadly falciparum. Without treatment for falciparum malaria, most people die; the fever skyrockets extremely high, doing internal damage to the body. This is the most dangerous type of malaria. Red blood cells infected with the parasite tend to sludge and form micro-infarctions (small areas of dead tissue due to lack of oxygen) in capillaries in the brain, liver, adrenal gland, intestinal tract, kidneys, lungs, and other organs. And of course, pregnant women, babies and children are the most vulnerable.

The second attack of malaria assaulted me in Lebangy. Hitting so quickly, I had no time to drive my truck to a hospital, as I would surely have failed along the way. I can only recount that malaria left me in a state of near delirium where I don't remember worrying about life and death. I don't remember being concerned that I was in such a remote part of the world, and so removed from medical help. I was in a different world. Thanks to my neighbors, I was taken care of and recovered. After the fever passed, I had a sense that during the sickness my mind had shut off, and turned all control over to my physical body to wage war with nature, hoping for survival. I couldn't remember conscious effort being put into this battle. It was a weird sense that there was no surplus energy for thought. It is a purely punishing, debilitating disease. I lost many pounds and my clothes would no longer fit. While recovering, I remember thinking how wonderful the human body is. Growing up in

Wisconsin I knew that the temperature outside the body could vary by up to 120 degrees and be fought off. But let the internal temperature of the body change by just 7 or 8 degrees, and a person is in serious trouble. Under that slight change, a body will not survive long. I was grateful mine had not gone quite that high.

One morning, Etienne, who worked with us, did not show for work. "Hey, Tsumbu, where's Etienne?" I asked.

"He's sick today."

"Yeah, what's he got?"

"Malaria."

I set the guys to work and left to check on Etienne, who had lost his wife at a young age and lived alone. He was a pleasant man, a good worker, but he was a gloomy sort, lonely I think. He had, for his own reasons, not married again, appearing to be in perpetual mourning for his lost companion. He was not given to laughter, even smiling seemed to cause him discomfort. Still I liked Etienne and was sad for his loneliness.

Although I had never been in his house before, I knew he would be unable to answer the door, so I knocked and quietly entered. There was no furniture in the one-room house; it was empty but for Etienne who was curled up on the dirt floor around a small fire that had died out. It was totally dark in the house as there were no windows and he had no kerosene lamp; the only light entered when the door was opened. But Etienne did not care; his battle was not about light. He was in the fever stage of malaria and barely aware of my presence.

"Do you want to go to the hospital?" I asked softly. He could barely move his head to motion no. "Can I get you water?" Again, by motion of his head, he answered no. He had no energy to move; he was deathly ill and just wanted to be left alone. But he would need water to hydrate himself for the great volume he would sweat out at night. Until I experienced the sweats of malaria, I had no idea the human body held so much fluid. A lot of weight can be lost in a bout of malaria but I wouldn't recommend associating with mosquitoes for that reason. I touched Etienne's forehead and noticed his fever was high. I had aspirin at home but could not give it to him; I had been made to understand that I was not to play doctor. Besides, we all assumed that a fever was malaria when there were other diseases with very similar symptoms.

In witnessing sicknesses and deaths I had become familiar with the universal language of touch to soothe the patient. It is the gentle rubbing on the shoulder, the gentle stroking of the head, the calm holding of a hand, and stroking the forearm. The receiver appreciates the companionship, comfort and connection to life. This had been done for me when I was sick and I understood its comfort to the sufferer. I did this for Etienne for a while, and then went back to work. I knew he would be checked on during the day as neighbors made sure he drank water. One of the reasons so many of the village's little children and babies died was the lack of re-hydration; they would not take in fluids nor understand why they should.

I knew that the outcome of Etienne's battle would now be determined by his body's ability to fight off nature. It was foreign and difficult for me to close the door of that mud walled room and leave someone who was suffering and could very well die, just lying in the dirt and darkness, alone. This would be pure, cold neglect at home and I felt this way as I left, but I could not and would not force him to go to the hospital. And there was no medical person, no medication, and no ambulance to call for help. Leaving him, I felt a coldness inside that made me shiver and feel guilty. But I had learned that some things are in no one's hands but the Good Lord's. Etienne eventually recovered, with no medication that I knew of. He remained a sad old man, however, never fully getting over losing his wife.

SUPERSTITIONS, OMENS, DRUGS AND THE RITE OF PASSAGE

CHAPTER EIGHTEEN

Ebanda Jean also worked with us on the school. He was a very sincere type, not one to create humor but he didn't mind a good laugh. He had a serious, intellectual side that he showed to us, a side that gave Tsumbu fuel for his comedy. A person could state a fact that he felt would forever enlighten the ages and be recorded in history, only to have Tsumbu tear that fact to rags and leave the world rolling in laughter. This frustrated Ebanda Jean for it was his intellectual side that he felt was his gift to the world. But Tsumbu was too sharp for him. Tsumbu was an antagonist to everything that appeared common logic: he would have been a great lawyer.

Jean was also one of the oldest of the "new generation" – the "post-French colonist generation." I realized this by his use of a Christian name. The unfortunate elders who had known the French never used Christian names; the missionaries had arrived too late to take advantage of, I mean, to save, their souls. This distinction in generations was stark in dress, language, acceptance of a new view of the outside world, and the deep desire to see it.

There was still a missionary. He would arrive periodically always dressed in his old, faded black robe, frayed where the hem had spent years scraping the ground of isolated jungle villages. He appeared to be held together by a knotted black, rope tied round his waist which some know as a rosary. As a boy I had been in school where this same rigging was worn. The deeply religious believed it a rosary and a sacrilege to abuse, but let the heads of the faithful turn for a split second and the less faithful would find the same instrument leaving welts on their sitting area! This missionary wore a severe, official manner and looked like a figure out of a history book. He'd come rumbling around in his worn out bush truck, kicking up dust and wearing a good part of it.

He came in search of recruits and to do some preaching. In listening to the missionary, Jean found his place in life; a comforting place for his mind and a belonging to something where he could shine and be acknowledged. It is a good feeling to see a person find the love and power of his soul and a cause to use it to better the world. After several years of study, Jean was being groomed to be a deacon in the church. He thrived on this mission and when he approached, his pride always arrived first; he glowed with it. Now I have to mention that, in my opinion, the missionary had an instinct to avoid Tsumbu. And wisely so, for he had met Tsumbu on previous visits and knew that any attempt at conversion could backfire and so shatter the foundations of his own beliefs that he'd be forced to put away the robes and take up the banjo.

While studying for the ministry, Jean continued to work on the school. He took pride in being a part of something so important for the village and understood the value of education. It was a typical day at the work site where conversation was light and friendly and the work progressed slowly. Slowly, by my standards, not theirs. Ebanda Jean's seventeen-year-old son, Ebanda Bartholomy, arrived home from Koula Moutou where he had attended high school. He was a handsome kid, athletic, a good student with a quiet, pleasant manner. We all greeted him warmly, Tsumbu asking if he had been expelled. In Jean's eyes you could see the love of a proud parent. A bit of small talk and Bartholomy went home to eat lunch; we would follow soon.

It was less than half an hour later when the calm, pace of the work site was destroyed by the screams of a voice in panic. " Jean, Ebanda Jean, come home! Ebanda Jean!" The plea was desperate. With the look of fear known only to parents, Jean dropped his tools and raced toward home. We were all shaken by the frantic cries.

The village burst to life, houses emptied, and barefoot villagers from everywhere began running in the direction of the screams. Screams, for these villagers, were the fire alarm, the tornado warning, and the civil defense siren. From the women came sounds that sounded like Alpine yodels gone mad. Word quickly got to us that Jean's son had gone home, eaten lunch and "just dropped dead!" There are times when the expected course of reality is so disturbed that a mind needs time to absorb the change. This happened that day. It is expected that the very sick and very old will die, but this was a healthy seventeen-year-old kid. How could he be living one moment and dead the next? The shock to the village was tremendous, and to Jean and his family, unspeakably heartbreaking. Even Tsumbu was quiet and absorbed in sadness. Groups formed throughout the village consoling and counseling each other. What was to happen next would have lasting effect on me; furthermore I would be forced to study my own culture for answers.

If someone unexpectedly drops dead, what happens next? At home, usually an autopsy is performed to reveal the cause of the tragedy. But this was not home, and I had to remember that I could not apply the American principles I grew up with to these people. I had to understand and respect their culture. These were a people who, in certain aspects of human development, seemed to parallel a time in the West before doctors were snatching bodies from graves in the darkness of night to clandestinely study their internal anatomy. A time before x-rays, before blood pressure screening, before autopsies, and most importantly, before Western medical professionals. I had to remember that, without external evidence of trauma, these people knew little about internal medicine. They had to rely on diagnoses that sounded right, mystical explanations, or the reading of the pattern of bones cast to the ground by a village doctor.

Therefore, there would be one theory that could never be proven but was believed, and it made many people suspect. Ebanda Bartholomy was young, healthy and had died just after eating lunch, so what was the most logical reason? Poison, of course! And not food poisoning, for there was no sign of sickness first, and this, they understood. Years of experience had taught them that certain foods make one sick and shouldn't be eaten. (I had been told to watch what the monkeys eat.) But this was an instant death and had to be intentional, as no mother would ever mistake a poisonous food as edible. But who did it and why?

Just as happens in America with the announcement that a crime has taken place, so it was there. Neighbor became suspicious of neighbor. Had someone gone mad? The easily frightened became temporarily paranoid. Everyone would suspiciously watch those close to the victim or anyone who might have reason to kill the victim. Was it the kid Bartholomy fought with two years ago? The old woman whose goat he had kicked? Was his father unhappy with him? Had his mother lost her mind? And how did the poison get in his food in his own house? It had to be someone he knew! Though not spoken publicly, these were the rumblings. But never was consideration given to a deadly medical experience; they could not consider a possibility they didn't know existed. I said nothing; it was neither my place nor the time for any suggestions about medical possibilities.

As at home in America, fears would eventually subside and rational thoughts would replace panic. The answer would be lost forever; there would be no proof unless given by a confession, which never came. Things would, in due course, calm down. However, what followed in the next several days sent me searching for some logic to explain the conundrum.

The body of Ebanda Jean's son lay on the dirt floor inside their home. I had to understand that there were no ambulances, no morgue, no casket makers, and that there would be no embalming. No thought would be given to taking the body to Koula Moutou, as burial would be there in the village. But it would be days before a funeral could be held. Word of this tragedy would have to be sent out by villagers walking to other villages. Those villagers would need time to prepare for the funeral and then more time to walk the trails to Lebangy. The body would lie on that dirt floor in that house until the day of the funeral. This meant the parents, and the brothers and sisters who witnessed the death, would now have to eat, sleep and live with their dead relative there on the floor!

I inquired as to why the body was not moved outside and was told that the animals would get it. There was nothing they could do and nothing that had been done for centuries except what I was seeing then. But this was the tropics - the temperature could push to 100 degrees and over! A body lying inside a house for days with no air circulation - a house where doors and windows were kept closed at night for safety- would cause the heavy odor which hung in the air to become unbearable. And when I was told several days later that the body was now lying in a puddle of its own decomposing fluids, my mind froze in disbelief. The casual, easy speech of the communicator spoke in a tone that said he had seen this a million times. To me, this was hideous! I had to think beyond my own disgust and disbelief to the family members who had to see their kin like this, who had to sleep each night with this horrible reality. How could they not be traumatized? How could they even sleep? Where were the counselors? There were none and none were needed. As a child back in America, it would have been beyond my comprehension to imagine this, but in this village the behavior was the natural, normal process for this event of life.

In time I would understand that the entire life cycle from birth to death would be experienced and witnessed by each individual in the village. No one was sheltered from seeing the sickness and dying of infants, the aged, and all those in-between. From birth and its first awareness, a child begins to participate in the life to death experience.

One stop along the life journey is when boys participate in a ceremony to become men. I was honored by an invitation to a very remote village, accessible only by footpath, to witness this "Rite of Passage" to manhood. After hours on foot along a narrow path beneath the impenetrable canopy that made the misty jungle dark, we arrived at a scene that had gone on for centuries. There was no evidence of modern technology anywhere, not even in general hardware such as nails. A large fire pit was blazing in the center of the tiny village of four or five mud homes, topped with grass roofs and hugged closely by the jungle. Tucked up close to and backed by the jungle, sat a small hut of stick walls and grass roof with only one entryway - no door - with an inside area about 8 feet by 10 feet. At night, an eerie light from the fire shot between the poled walls, reflecting off the eyes and bodies of those passing on the opposite side.

A group of eleven boys were to make their passage to become men. During the Bowiti ceremony, which would last 60 hours straight, these boys would be kept awake and active. A hallucinogenic bark was eaten and the boys were kept busy dancing around and through the fire – which connected them with the ancestral spirit world. Alternating with the dancing were lectures in the hut. At first it seemed like kind of a "whoopee" celebration, but as this ceremony was explained to me, I understood the meaning, one that meant survival for the culture, and the warriors that protect that culture.

These boys consumed hallucinogenic bark, drank palm wine (pleasing to the taste and warming to the heart), and danced around the fire, chanting and singing in communication with the ancestors. Between dances the boys heard lectures of wisdom from highly regarded and respected elders who passed on their life experiences as men, fathers, husbands, grandfathers, and community members. They also passed on the customs and history of their culture, and stories of men who had come and gone. Next, there was more vision producing bark and dancing, voices now chanting with an obvious attempt to be the deep, masculine voices of men. After that, more lectures from the fathers who explained how to be a husband and a father, how to provide food and shelter for a family, and what social responsibilities they had to the village. Then followed more dancing around the fire with their ancestors, the chants sounding deeper now, more lectures on life, including how to make love to a woman and care for a wife. More dancing and chanting accompanied by a pulsating tempo of thundering drums pounded to create a force in the air. This power combined with the shadows darting about, reflecting off faces and the jungle walls, created a vibrating energy that transfixed the village. They continued straight through the day and night.

After two and a half days, these exhausted boys, now well educated in life's expectations and well lubricated with palm wine and hallucinogenic barks, were lined up naked. Two men approached; one holding what appeared to be a honed, flattened piece of steel for a scalpel, the other carrying a clay bowl of ashes. Stopping in front of each boy, the man with the knife reached down and pulled the foreskin of the penis forward and circumcised the boy. The second man took the circumcised penis and dipped it in the ashes to cauterize the wound. Not at all a simple act, but one holding deep importance and possibly eternal humiliation. A simple movement, a crying out, a slight twitch and a boy would forever be considered unworthy of becoming a man, and drift in a state between manhood and boyhood unable to identify with or be accepted by either. Nor would this boy-man be allowed to marry; he would be forever isolated on the outskirts of the village.

This group of eleven boys made the journey to become eleven men. It was later explained to me that the days of grueling dancing and chanting, the hallucinogenic bark, the wine and, of course, the lectures were designed as a safeguard to the longevity of the culture. Worn out and drugged, these boys were too exhausted to flinch. This was explained to me in humor because, I was told, without the fatiguing ceremony, there would be few men left in their culture. However, the importance of this ceremony to the survival of the culture was easily understood.

I wondered about boys back home. Many American boys would pass that great moment to manhood with their fathers by sharing their first beer together. Some sort of a rite of passage, but definitely not all a boy needed to know to become a man. As a culture, did we have a ceremony outside of the first beer with dad? How many were taught the physical beauty of making love to a woman, what to expect as a husband, father, grandfather, the responsibilities as head of a household, and so forth? I could think of no one who had received this information. Most had learned it on the streets by their own experimentation. I have seen so many marriages in this country that received no counseling until so much damage has been done that the marriage is doomed. Then the professional world wants to help the crippled covenant. Sad! Who is more advanced?

What about fatherhood? Should these fundamental, experiences of life be left to chance? How foolish we seem. Why be ashamed to talk about these things? There, in Africa, they were so much better at this. How much enjoyment we miss in life because we don't communicate the truth, the beautiful truth.

I had not had a rite of passage at age eleven. And when I had turned twenty-one, "legally" old enough to drink alcohol, I had been in Vietnam. It was May 19, the day before my birthday. We were high up in the central highland mountains and the day had been typically sweltering; we were soaked in sweat and exhausted from physical and mental strains. One day earlier we had been re-supplied with food, water, and mail, and in our re-supply, we each received two cans of coke and one can of beer. After bartering, those who drank soda had traded off their cans of beer and vice versa.

I had saved one can of beer and it was there in my backpack that day, taking in all the heat and shaking of our mountainous climb. I remembered from the Boy Scout Manual that if you buried something 18 inches or so in the ground and left it overnight, it would be cool – not cold – but cool. I decided to bury this can of beer in preparation for my own rite of passage into manhood the following day. I slept that night and awoke to manhood! What a glorious day! But why did I not feel a whole lot different than the day before? I was given no secrets of exalted manhood, tribal introduction to husbanding, how to make love to a woman, what to expect as a father, or my duties to society. I was only given orders to "get ready to move out." Another day of war, looking to kill before being killed. I didn't have time for manhood just then. I was more concerned that my weapon was clean and ready to save my life; that my gear was properly packaged. Just enough time for a few deep thoughts of my friend and sweetheart, a last puff on a cigarette, and a wish that I were at a bar back home to celebrate the big "21" with my buddies, drinking shots, and acting stupid – the usual atmosphere to pass into manhood in America! Instead I had to make do with one cool can of buried beer; at least I was still alive to celebrate and took advantage of a few seconds to dig up my beer, and motion by hand for a buddy to come help me celebrate. I retrieved the can, pulled the tab and whoosh! A spout of foam spewed into the air. With the lifeblood of manhood escaping, I desperately shoved the can to my mouth to trap as much of the rite of passage as I could choke down. I then reburied the can, just a few inches this time, so the Viet Cong wouldn't cut it into shrapnel and use the pieces in a booby trap and kill me with my own rite of passage vessel.

The important ceremony of passage to manhood complete, I picked up my machine gun and backpack and moved out with the platoon. Funny though, that rite of passage hadn't seemed to change me much; that day was just another fear-filled trudge looking for trip wires, booby traps and men "of the enemy". Being at war was a passage into manhood for me and many others, but it taught so many wrong things and didn't explain the right ones in a way any of us could understand. Seeing the rite in Africa let me know what I had gained and how much more we need to tell our boys so they may become men.

WHEN NATURE KILLS

CHAPTER NINETEEN

There was no medical treatment in our village; the nearest hospital was 35 kilometers away in Koula Moutou. During the monsoon season with bridges washed away and roads impassible, it might as well have been 1000 kilometers away. I could provide transportation during the dry season, but several aggravating hurdles often prevented this. Most of the adults were afraid of the truck and would not get in it. Even worse, many were horrified of the hospital and the white doctors. They chose to stay home and take their chances with family, familiarity and traditional medicine. I wondered how much of this was lingering fear of the French colonists who had not displayed the compassion needed for the villagers to become confident in them.

Nothing brought me closer to heartache than the diseases in young children. Of these, the most wrenching were the diseases of infants. It seemed most babies born in the village would face death before learning to crawl. Mothers not long removed from their own childhood, and doing nothing different than all their mothers and grandmothers before them at ages thirteen through sixteen, were giving birth. This was quite normal and expected at these ages.

Many of these young mothers would appear at my door clutching a tiny bundle in their arms. I quickly learned what these bundles held but never got accustomed to seeing what was about to be uncovered. Folding back the worn out cloth (one my own mother would long ago have given to the rag man), the mother exposed a chilling sight, hardly recognizable as human. There was the haunting, emaciated face with skin drawn so tightly to bone that it appeared a vacant skull. Sunken, lifeless eyes stared in motionless emptiness, never blinked, and there was no longer energy to cry. I knew these eyes and the dying spirit behind them; they were my eyes as I appeared in that photo after war when my own, dying spirit viewed the world with the 1000-yard stare. But this was a baby with no life experience and yet the same empty gaze. I realized that I had known spirit only by human definition and was experiencing something different; I had been out of touch with true spirit. I knew this child had yet to learn to walk, but how could I claim wisdom to understand the spirit of this baby? I could not and yet I sensed a connection, a deep respect and desperation to help this little spirit, as I had once been desperate to help my own. It is urgency from the spirit that drives us in desperation to save the body.

An adult when sick can be forced to take fluids, but not a baby. The baby will have none of the liquids offered, and cannot understand it must replenish its body to survive. "My baby is very sick, can you take me to the hospital in Koula Moutou?" I had been taught to communicate with the animals and most importantly, watch the body language, and had learned to regard this same communication in humans. I had come to believe that humans do more communicating with body language than spoken words. And so it was with this young mother when she spoke that simple sentence. Her body – especially her eyes – spoke desperately, and with a passion of heartbreak. The spirit expressing itself through the body what we need to connect with.

It was diarrhea that made these babies sick, but the dehydration was what they were dying from. The people did not always know the connection between diarrhea and dehydration. I had heard that women, while nursing an infant, would not have intercourse with a man as it was their belief that the man's sperm would enter the mother's milk and kill the baby; a rational explanation when they did not understand the world of bacteria and the microscopic world of disease. I would encounter many such beliefs that explained their world, but I criticized none for I might have come to many of the same conclusions without my American education.

Only an intravenous replacement of fluids could save the lives of these sick babies, and that could only be administered at the hospital in Koula Moutou. Everything was dropped to get these babies to the hospital but there is no adequate expression for emotions felt when the monsoon season left the road impassable and the deaths of these infants inevitable. The number of babies that died from this easily treated condition is staggering. I am not qualified to speak of the devastation to these young mothers, but felt it was no less devastating than for a mother at home in America.

The frequency of this condition in infants had a deep influence on me, and the topic was recurrent in conversations I had with Michael, an American English teacher at the school in Koula Moutou. A plan grew out of these conversations that seemed so simple and logical I wondered why we had taken so long to realize the possibility. We both believed that the bacteria causing the diarrhea were carried in food and drinking water, or in many cases the containers these were stored or served in. If we could prove that these bacteria, invisible to the eye, were in fact present in the food and water, and that these same bacteria were responsible for diseases, the villagers would be armed with facts to improve health conditions dramatically. This revelation would save lives and decrease the infant death rate. Michael borrowed a microscope from his school's lab, and brought it to our village in the bush to prove the existence of deadly bacteria in the water. We were both excited and confident that great changes in health awareness were about to save the continent of Africa!

Michael focused in the microscope, then filled a glass jar with water provided by one of the three villagers invited to participate. He held the jar of water before him and delivered his opening address: "You cannot see them, but there are little animals in this water that can kill you!" No experiment has ever fallen apart as rapidly and completely as ours! The three men stood frozen before us, with heads lowered and eyes straining to look up under eyebrows at us. We had convinced them of only one thing, that we were lunatics!

"Well, how do you know there are animals in there if you can't see them?" one of the men asked.

Michael went on to prove our lunacy when he made a slide and slid it onto the table of the microscope. "Here! Look in here, you can see them!" I watched quietly as not a man moved; all three remained rigid and motionless except for their eyes straining left and right in their sockets, desperately trying to catch a quick glimpse of each others' eyes to see if each thought we were as insane as the other thought. Then slowly, each man moved forward to take a chance and look down the barrel of this thing he could make no sense of, politely backed away and with courtesy nodded politely that yes, he had looked inside. But only blank expressions answered Michael's question, "Did you see the animals?" After a few moments, Michael looked at me and I at him. No words were needed for the two of us to fall into the laughter of our own folly. This laughter released the tension being suffered by our three students, who also fell to laughter. They seemed relieved that they were not in the presence of dangerous madmen, and that whatever it was we were doing was all in the name of good-natured fun and not black magic put on them. Michael and I laughed at realizing that these men had no reason to understand magnification, microscopes, nor the relationship of the test slide to the magnifying lens and the eye.

Once again the collision of cultures had met an impasse and

although we had done nothing to improve the health of Africa, we had all enjoyed a good laugh, but for different reasons. The men anxiously departed and are no doubt still recounting to neighbors the weird customs and traditions of America!

I do believe, however, and without humor, that this lack of understanding of the microscopic world of bacteria and viruses for remote peoples is in part why some diseases are so prolific in Africa. As we provide education to the children, they will gain the information needed to understand the meaning of small creatures swimming around in their water.

FOLLIES OF JUDGEMENT, JOYS OF FORGIVENESS

CHAPTER TWENTY

Drenched in sweat, skin crusted in dirt, exhausted and slumped under the weight of our rucksacks, we emerged from the central highland mountains of Vietnam; a much deserved break from days of hunting the Vietcong, sleeping on the jungle floor like rodents, and the constant vigilance to spot "them" before they spotted us. We walked onto the firebase and dropped to the ground on the first open space we found, using our rucksacks now as back rests. Among the sighs of relief and other, more profane expressions that reflected the general attitude of life there I heard a quiet voice nearby mumble, "there goes Goofy Grape." I was laughing at the name when I turned my head slowly to catch sight of a very tall, slender black soldier passing by. Beneath the sweat I could see a man so very black his skin had a purple shine to it. He too was slumped from the weight on his back and fatigue, and used his green, Army-supplied towel over his shoulders to keep the straps of his rucksack from digging into his skin. I felt ashamed to be laughing, but I was not laughing at this man. I was laughing, in my own fatigue, remembering the crazy, spastic looking grape character on the packages of Kool-Aid who was named Goofy Grape.

This man did not deserve the comment from these idiots; he was an E-6 Staff Sergeant. Staff Sergeants, E-7 Sergeants First Class, Lieutenants, and Captains led the war in the jungle and I respected them. I felt guilty for the appearance of laughing at this man whose name I did not know and who served in a different platoon. It would be only a short time later that I would hear he died in combat crawling forward on his belly to help a wounded soldier.

Witnessing the shallowness of people like this taught me to deal in souls and spirits. I believe to notice a person by skin and not by spirit is to miss something very important in life. I am sure that African American sergeant had family that he loved and who loved him, and were just as heartbroken at their loss as the loved ones of fallen Hispanic, Native American, Asian and white soldiers. I would have thought that definition by skin color or culture would have long ago been set aside in life as pure foolishness. But the world is made up of all kinds of people – those who are determined to undermine others because of differences, and those who are determined to help others, seeing only similarities in human nature.

I was reminded of this when Tsumbu told me how his dying mother had been carried through the jungle on a makeshift stretcher to get medical help from a "great white doctor." While recounting this, Tsumbu was pointing at a small footpath leaving the village and disappearing into the jungle. "But that's west, there is nothing but dense jungle for hundreds of kilometers!" "I know," he said, "it's l-l-l-ooo-nng from here," as if stretching out the spoken word gave scale to the impressive distance. "It took days," he said. I was not sure if Tsumbu's mom, who was sister to the chief, was sent to the great white doctor by medical need or social station. I did not ask that question.

The conversation passed but the subject left a burning curiosity as I looked toward the jungle and wondered who could be out there. My curiosity burned; I had to know. Some weeks or months later, I would again hear of this man but now with a name attached: Dr Schweitzer was the name and Lamberene the site of his hospital. By my map, they walked almost 250 kilometers, and this through some of the most dense, uninhabited jungle in the world; their only company the treacherous wild life and more deadly insects. But this jungle was their home, too, and they were perfectly prepared to be there. But my mind could not escape this thought: this was over 150 miles on foot to see a doctor! I had to be impressed by this extraordinary example of human devotion to a loved one, and determination to do whatever it took to get help.

I planned to seek out this Dr. Schweitzer, of whose name I seemed to have a vague recollection, but from where and why I could not say. On my next trip to the capital, I would swing south at the fork in the road at Bifoun rather than north to Libreville, and head to Lamberene to track down this man whose name had long ago penetrated deep into the jungle and landed reverently on the lips of some of the most remote folks in the world, without radio, television or mail service. With his name now on my lips, I was anxious to meet this man who most certainly would share my love and passion for life there; we would have so much to talk about.

My discovery in Lamberene gave me a grieving sense of loss as I learned that Dr. Albert Schweitzer, the great white doctor, had died in 1965 at age ninety, more than a dozen years earlier. He was buried, alongside his wife, at his beloved hospital where he had spent a half-century dedicated to serving life. I felt cheated, there would not be hours of fascinating conversation and sharing experiences.

But a short time at his hospital made me realize I was in the after-presence of a great, great man. He was still very much there, alive and communicating with me. His spirit was everywhere - in the buildings, in the air and especially in the people continuing his work there at his exceptional hospital. I needed only to look and listen to hear the great doctor speak through the manifestations of his work.

Marie, a Gabonese nurse who had worked with Dr. Schweitzer, greeted me. Marie was a short, stout woman with beautiful snow-white hair that caused a remarkable contrast to the deep blackness of her skin. She offered me a warm, welcoming smile and with loving eyes, said, "I am happy you are here to visit us and I am excited to show you around."

Marie was the perfect choice to represent the hospital and Dr. Schweitzer. As she led me on a tour of the grounds, I was captivated by her gentle, reverent words explaining the history and continuing work of the hospital. Her voice reflected her love and admiration for the great doctor, the hospital and her own contribution to that wonderful place there in the jungle. She also introduced me to the philosophy of Dr. Schweitzer that won him the Nobel Peace Prize in 1952. "Reverence for life" was his mantra for all life, not just human life. Having been to war, I was immediately struck by this statement; it would cause deep reflection about the effects on my spirit from participating in the destruction of life during war, and building schools in Africa to improve life. It has been said that to preach his philosophy is easy but the proof of his belief in that reverence for life was best expressed by the hospital he built and the devotion he gave to it for half a century. I agree.

On the tour I was shown Dr. Schweitzer's living quarters, now maintained as a museum of sorts. The room was stark, simple and void of most western comforts: there was a bed with mosquito netting, kerosene lantern, piano, and his desk, on top of which rested his eyeglasses. I was moved as I stared at those glasses, knowing the great doctor had actually touched and worn them; this was a connection to the living man that warmed me.

When Marie spoke of Dr. Schweitzer's love for the music of Bach, and how he would play it on the old piano - well loved by use - I was mesmerized. I could not resist the thoughts of the African Jungle hearing the Brandenburg Concerto for the first time; this extraordinary sound floating over the jungle, insect and elephant, monkey and hippopotamus, snake and antelope, and of course the people. I would have loved to have had a ticket to that first performance!

I realized by the rustic room and simple furnishings that I did not need to ask Marie if she thought Dr. Schweitzer had missed the comforts of Europe. I lived in similar conditions there in Africa and was well aware that fine furniture, all that electricity allowed, running water, and the endless list of material possessions desired in America were of no importance to one who knows that happiness in the soul is the only true possession of value.

Dr. Schweitzer had traveled 100 miles up the Ogouee River in the early 1900s. With no electric power or amenities of the day, he had carved his hospital out of a forbidding jungle to live amidst the malaria, sleeping sickness, leprosy and many other diseases; definitely a man with an unselfish heart and soul dedicated to making life better for the Africans. There would never be a shortage of life to make better there for during my short visit I saw the pirogues, dugout canoes, arrive on the banks of the Ogouee River, transporting more patients from somewhere deeper in the jungle. And I knew sadly that this procession of sick and dying would continue to arrive by footpath and this centuries old river transportation for many, many years to come. I knew also that this was only a tiny percent of those suffering and dying deep in remote jungle villages, many of whom would never reach this place of hope and comfort. But for those who did, they would find the spirit of Dr. Albert Schweitzer and his reverence for life waiting to help.

People like the young African American sergeant who lost his life in Vietnam while trying to help another, Dr. Albert Schweitzer, and all who are munificent in giving of themselves, are the real heroes of this world.

When I returned home to America, it was by extraordinary circumstance that the book, *A Treasury of Albert Schweitzer* would come to me at a desperate time, revealing several short sentences that lifted the veil of darkness that was again haunting my soul. He has continued speaking profoundly to me for years, and through his writings has become one of the most influential people in my life.

ON DEATH, DYING AND LIFE

CHAPTER TWENTY-ONE

While in Africa, I had been so absorbed in the fascinations of life that seldom did the pain of war come to mind. At least, not long enough to focus on. However, there was always something rumbling in my mind. Africa's intrigues helped to keep the rumblings quiet, but I was aware of them from time to time.

There were so many beautiful parts to life in the village where I lived. The elders, or those too old to work in the jungle, were left to the chores of babysitting and watching the village. There are no old-age homes in Africa, at least, not where I was at that time. The elders were respected, if for no other reason than they had lived long and were entitled to retired life with dignity. They remained an important part of family and village life. Even those elders afflicted with senility were revered and given shelter, food and attention. They belonged and were cared for. The elders also helped pass down history and the wisdom of their people. I spent many hours sitting around a fire entranced by their stories and knowledge.

The children that were too young to work in the jungle plantations were left to play in the village. Kids with handicaps of any sort were not put away in homes, were not hidden from society. They belonged and were accepted. Life was not cleansed of "imperfections"; life was not cleansed of people who were "not whole." They were all considered an important part of life, and not a life dictated by who should walk the streets and who should not. I remember a man who lived near a fork in the main road, one leg of the road going to Lastorsville and one leg to another village. This man would stand at that fork in the road all day and repeat those village names and nothing more. He would face one direction and repeat, "Lastorsville, Lastorsville, Lastorsville," and then switch and start saying, "Koula-Moutou, Koula-Moutou, Koula-Moutou." For hours he would do this and speak no other words. But he was not dangerous and was left alone. Life was lived with him in it, not him hidden from life.

The market places in the larger villages were not just places to buy food and necessary items but also to socialize. Even the price of goods was bartered as a social activity more than a simple purchase. And here, those afflicted would also live life; the crippled, those people with birth defects, the blind – they were all part of society and left to enjoy life as they could. This would be so unacceptable in America. We want to see only normal and normal is not what nature makes, normal is what people dictate is acceptable.

America is on a rampage to ensure the perfect appearance of the human body. If it's not perfect, hell, just fill it with silicone, or suck the fat out, or lift, tuck and tighten the skin. We can't get enough of our cosmetic overhauls! And for those who can't keep up or can't afford these overhauls, there are alcohol, drugs and anti-anxiety medicine, and more than enough food to soothe the fears of not being perfect. America seems to be on a fast ride to physical perfection and advertising makes its role enhancing that goal. For those who can't keep up, they surrender their souls to anxiety and just admire those who can, envy others and suffer the loss of self-esteem and self-respect that goes with envy. And if you are old and retired or have physical disabilities, stay out of the way of those who want their money, their material goods, their silicone and skin suction, and their possessions!

In America, we have homes for the elderly and homes or special places for the handicapped or orphaned children. We don't want to see these people – put them away! We do this at the expense of knowing that many of the elderly receive poor care, are robbed, and are abused in these homes. We know children are molested in some day care centers as well as orphanages. Many just close their eyes, think it can't happen to their families, and continue about the business of making money and having things. Grandparents are even suing in court just to see their grandchildren. Kids are committing unheard of crimes, yet nobody can stop the fast train to materialistic goals that most people are on. "Keep those people out of our lives; we don't have time for them," has become the implicit mantra of many Americans.

I loved the social structure in that village tucked away in the jungle. The process of life and aging was of importance at every age. It was beautiful to see. This would help repair my soul in years to come; help to solve a piece of the puzzle. During this time and the six-month extension I added to the original two years (I did not want to leave), I was absorbed into village life. I knew the absorption was complete when a truck came into the village one day carrying three Europeans. The truck's appearance alone brought much attention. The three Europeans brought more. They had come in search of art and artifacts –drums, masks and the like. They announced their intentions to the chief through a younger interpreter. Those villagers who had artifacts brought them out. I was standing in front of my house with the chief's nephew, my good friend Tsumbu, who had a great sense of humor. I knew Tsumbu no longer regarded me by my skin color when he blurted out, "Oh, Les Blance son fou!" ("Oh, the whites are fools!") He explained to me that whites have been going to Africa for many decades to hunt and collect artifacts. So as not to disappoint them and make a few bucks in the deal, the people would carve masks and drums and statues, bury them in the ground for six months to a year and Voila!

antique artifacts, sufficiently aged and cured, worm holes and all! It worked every time - instant antiques. How we laughed as the Europeans made their purchases of these "valuable" items.

I wonder to this day how many pieces of this kind of "African art" are on display around the world represented as authentic. Yes they are authentic! Authentic fakes. There is such a sense of sadness concerning this, for if greedy artifact gatherers would pay attention to the beauty of the African people and their cultures, they would perhaps realize the deep importance these masks, drums and artifacts represent. They would see the connection these people have to their ancestral world, and the energy and spirit of all life that they respect and to which they are so deeply connected.

Another incident I remember quite distinctly is when an American doctor, dispatched by the Department of State and sent to Africa to provide Peace Corp volunteers and other American personnel with medical treatment, came out to our village. The poor guy was so drunk he could hardly speak. While attempting to collect a schistosomiasis sample, the drunken fool fell in the river and had to be dragged to dry land. I was so ashamed before the villagers that this man represented the important medical healers from my country; he was an embarrassing buffoon. Here was a beautiful opportunity to study the natural healers and their medicines, but he was too polluted and arrogant to find any value in that "low medicine." I wondered at his dismay when he was relieved of service and sent back to the States where he belonged. He could have learned so much! It reminded me of how egocentric and materialistic some American doctors can be and I wondered if they have taken a Hippocratic oath or a Hypocrites' oath? Why are their fees so outrageous? Is their goal to heal or to have money?

I was, after a time, allowed to participate as a villager in different ceremonies, weddings and funerals, especially. Weddings were happy events – drum playing, colorful dancing and singing. Funerals were almost like weddings; drummers, singing and dancing, but, the singing was more dirge like, sad. But there was much tradition behind these events. As I became accustomed to life in Lebangy, I noticed events that stood out clearly. Here was society stripped of all, or most all, materialism. It was bare, beautiful life lived with the clutter of wants removed. One witnessed the cycle of life from birth to death. No matter the age, one was witness to life. There in the village, one was born, lived and died, aware of each phase of life and witnessing the aging and dying process. Mourning was natural.

I am fourth oldest of ten children and I remember my mother being pregnant with the younger ones. When the time for a new birth arrived, my ma was whisked off to the hospital. She and my dad saw the birth process. We, as kids, were not allowed in the hospital. I remember my dad taking us to visit. We would stand outside the hospital and wave at my mother through her hospital window. There in Africa, a woman gave birth at home and the children could watch the bloody birth taking place, could hear the moans of pain. They understood the event. My ma went to the hospital and came home several days later with a new brother or sister, all clean and bundled in blankets. I had witnessed nothing. Hell, I never even saw the stork! I wondered about this while living in Africa as the children there witnessed much more concerning birth than I ever had.

The children in the village also witnessed the dying process. They would watch the elderly get sick and die in their homes. They would watch all ages of people dying from disease or accident, and they were not traumatized by death. They also had realistic beliefs in the hereafter. In America, we are sheltered from the end of life. Our religions terrify us with death, its fire and eternal torment. We have little experience with dying and death. It is done in the hospital out of our sight. We have no comfortable idea of the hereafter except horrifying fears and cemeteries.

Is this a part of trauma of war? That life can end so quickly at such an early age and with no other belief than fear of the afterlife and punishment eternal? Why doesn't our society have a different approach to death that would, be comforting? God has assured us that a great hereafter exists but mankind has created its own panicky fears of that event. Why are cemeteries so frightening and spooky to us? After all, there was a time in Europe when cemeteries were social gathering places. People courted in the cemeteries. Vendors sold bread and knickknacks in the cemeteries. Executive documents were not official until read aloud in a cemetery. The death sentence of Joan of Arc could not be carried out until the official document was read in the public forum of the cemetery. When did this change to a dread fear of death? My own fear of my death was definitely a huge part of the trauma I suffered in war. After all, in combat the most consuming instinct is to stay alive: Kill them before they kill you. And believe it or not, this thought superseded all thoughts of baseball, apple pie, the flag, and saving the homeland.

In later years, I searched for an understanding of death and dying. I learned that as recently as the 1920s, 30s, and 40s, people were more familiar with death. It was not uncommon for extended families to live together - children, parents and grandparents. In those years, many types of diseases afflicted young and old. The infant mortality rate was very high in America in the early 1900s. It was common for the sick to remain at home where the doctor would actually come to the house to treat them. It was common for a child or young adult to watch a brother or sister, a parent or grandparent get sick, be treated at home, and in many cases, die at home. They watched the life cycles of their loved ones. They experienced death. Children watched their parents grieve and share emotions and these children participated in that grieving and death experience.

I remember how back in Africa the son of Ebanda Jean had died, and his body lay decomposing in the tropical heat on the floor of their home for several days awaiting the funeral guests and the barbaric wonder I had had about it. I would learn that in America as recently as the 1930's this very same thing happened here. Funeral homes did not come into existence in America until then. Right here in America it was common for a family member to die at home and the body lay in the home for days, awaiting a funeral. The embalmer would actually come to the home with his "cooling boards" to perform his work. And the wake and funeral would be held there in the home, often using the dining room table to lay out the body for services. And imagine the odor in the house on a hot summer day! But think of this, Americans, children and adults, were accustomed to sleeping at night with a dead body in the house. They would get up for breakfast and consider it normal to see a dead family member (of any age) in their company.

I have read how in the early 1900s, families would actually pack a lunch and the whole gang go off to watch the public hanging of criminals. It was a social event. Imagine this death experience for children and adults. Teddy Roosevelt, the great warrior and big game hunter, threatened to cancel college football because of the violent injuries and deaths. In 1905 alone, eighteen college players were killed, many seriously injured; some avid fans of today may realize that the forward pass was developed to stem these tragic deaths. But death was a part of the life experience then and the sport, despite the deaths, was growing in popularity. We can't even imagine watching this type of death take place today.

In the 1940s more than 40 percent of Americans lived on farms. I recall how in Africa the hunters would return from the jungle with their catch. The children would gather round in curiosity, drop to their haunches, and watch as the animal was gutted, skinned, decapitated, and cut up. They would see the blood drain. But more amazingly, their curiosity did not contain a queasy stomach, but rather the hopes of getting a small portion of meat to take home. The process was simply normal. I would watch with these children as a gorilla would be cut open and the organs exposed and removed. The hunter would take the heart or another organ, put that bloody, wet organ into a kid's hands and tell him or her, "Get this, take it to your mom." Or the hunter might simply cut off a leg or arm and with fur still attached, hand it over as I watched a five or six or seven year old excitedly racing off, toting the hairy limb with enthusiasm for the great gift.

One day I was outside my house in Africa. It was a funeral day and special preparations were being made in the village for the event. As usual, the kids were out playing. A neighbor approached, leading a goat on a braided rope. He stopped beneath a small tree, tied a rope from the tree to the goat's rear legs, and casually raised the frantically bucking, crying animal off the ground. With the kids gathering around as curious kids do, the man took his knife and with a quick flash slit the goat's throat. Blood gushed everywhere; the goat madly and wildly flailed about in mid air urinating and defecating uncontrollably, a hideous, haunting gurgling sound coming from the slashed throat as it choked on blood. When the goat was dead and hanging limp, the kids walked away, their posture saying, "That was cool. What'd ya wanna play now?"

I believe this experience with death was once more familiar to Americans. But with fewer then 3 percent of people now living on farms, and laws that imprison abusers of animals, and remove violence from daily life, I wonder if people even make a connection between the meats they see in grocery stores and live animals. I believe these interactions with the death experience and their removal from our life experience help to make the trauma of war more severe. I know this to be true because some military units require new soldiers to break the neck of a live chicken to give the soldier some minute connection to this thing called death. Although it is an isolated introduction to the death experience, it neglects one profound truth – chickens don't carry wallets with photos of loved ones!

Life in America changed drastically in the late 1950's and 1960's. Doctors no longer make house calls, the sick are taken to hospital, dying usually happens in the hospital or a nursing home. The infirm of mind are held in asylums. Those with handicaps are only recently getting their legal rights to public access after years of being institutionalized for physical (not mental) handicaps. Our society has, in its own way, designed itself to see only what is healthy and gloss over what is not considered "normal." This is causing suffering and anxiety called "fear of death." It is behind the idea that the military should not share the horrors of war with those at home. Those at home are somehow too fragile. Yet, how can our veterans regain their balance by going good when they are too ashamed of what they have done too share with the ones they need to be close to? As with all who go to war, the denial of death had its effect on me and on my family who awaited my return from Vietnam.

For now, I will say Africa is the only balance I found for my soul. After several years I would return home to the States with a wealth of experience that would help much later when my PTSD became devastatingly severe.

NATURE RETALIATES ON ME

CHAPTER TWENTY-TWO

Under the oppressive midday heat of the dry season I, as most villagers, lay as lifeless as possible. There was no activity, the village made no sounds, even the goats took to shade; it was just too hot.

I was floating lazily in my hammock and had drifted away in my thoughts to escape the heat when, "Ouch! What the hell was that?" I yelled this, not in my hammock, but in mid-air where a sharp stab in the back had sent me. On landing I caught sight of my assailant as a huge tsetse fly navigated out from behind me. A bite from a tsetse fly is not an insect bite, it's an attack with a deadly weapon and painful. "SOB, I'll get you!" I threatened, but it was too quick and disappeared.

Within days, the lively nematodes resulting from that bite began to devour the flesh beneath the skin of my back and migrate through it as they multiplied. Huge puss-filled lumps appeared, covering my entire back and shoulders. I was experiencing a parasitic relationship that I had only read about in science class, and I was not the parasite. These tiny invading nematodes appeared to be having the time of their lives at my inconvenience. I could feel their endless activities as they crawled around in my flesh. This caused no end of discomfort in the way of itching that got so aggravating I wanted to rip the skin off my back to get relief. And do you think they had the courtesy to work in shifts and let me sleep nights? They were untiring in their appetite; I slept little and could not lie on my back. I had an eerie sense knowing that I was supporting a colony of foreign life that had no apparent regard for mine, except to consume it. And I had no idea what their intentions were. Would they take over my entire body? Would they assault my chest, legs, and face? What if they got into my organs? How much of me would they be satisfied to devour? No villagers were familiar with this disease; they had never seen this before. This deeply concerned me. If they had no knowledge of this disease, who would? I was deep in the bush, a long way from medical help. Having yet to warm up to the skills of the traditional doctor and his professional opinion, and without much desire to do this at the moment, I packed up, pointed my bush truck north on the dirt road toward the capital, and took off.

The American university educated doctor at the hospital in Libreville was stumped. He threw up his hands and suggested I return to the States. Angry, I thought, "This is great, I don't want to go back to the States!" The drone of all those feelings of anger, emptiness and anxiety left by war began to rumble. But I had no choice, go home or be eaten alive by nematodes - the name itself was disgusting. What do you put on a tombstone for that one?

The disease equally confounded the pathologist for the Department of State in Washington, D.C. His biopsies found no clues, and by now, I had become truly concerned. This pathologist was billed as one of the best; he specialized in infectious diseases from around the world. When he was out of ideas, I felt tremendously low. When he surrendered to the nematodes and sent me home to Milwaukee, I was near bottom for answers. In anguish and discomfort as host to these miniature barbarians that were slowly devouring my very flesh, I now had to think there would be no cure. The damned nematodes would win and all I could do was sit and be their food source. And, I would have nothing to say about it as I was out-voted and out-numbered. If I had let my imagination wander, I could have created horror movies of these nematodes and their destruction. The mind will create defeating ideas if left to wander free, but war had taught me to deal in realities and not be haunted by my own imagination.

In situations like this some people feel compelled to enlighten others by saying such things as "Look at the bright side!" But this is usually said by people who are on the bright side. It doesn't help much for the one in the dark. But I suppose there was a bright side. While these nematodes were aggravating, uninvited companions and I could go nowhere without them, they didn't play loud music.

I returned to Milwaukee and was admitted to the small county hospital. But what doctor in Milwaukee could find what a world-renowned tropical disease specialist and pathologist could not? I was depressed that I would never again see Africa, but more frightening, I knew that I would return to my personal darkness. The unexplainable emptiness created during the devastations of war would be waiting.

In Milwaukee, Dr. Michael Dailey, specializing in infectious diseases, accepted the challenge. He took it up with great enthusiasm and tireless investigation, never quitting. For days he poked around my back taking biopsies and wearing out reference books. These now arrogant nematodes, thinking they had beaten the medical world's best doctors, had to be stunned when the news hit. With his white medical frock whipping in his wake as he flew into the room, his face beaming with the excitement of all great discoveries, he exclaimed, "I got them!" Smiling broadly, he declared, "We know what you have!"

Now, one would think the sufferer (me) would be given the floor to rejoice, but not in this situation. There was no way I could rejoice as much as Dr. Dailey. He had found that "something" in himself that is more valuable than money and possessions, the one thing that most humans either consciously or otherwise search for – a purpose in life – a raison d'être. That one activity that says, "Yes, this is what I love, this is the purpose of my life, this is a reason to be." And the person who has found this purpose cannot hide it, cannot control its glow because it shines naturally. Dr. Dailey was a great example that this purpose could exist and gave me hope. I must state that I was happy for Dr. Dailey, and enjoyed the enthusiasm and excitement that burst from him. After all, he had discovered in Milwaukee not just a disease arrived from Africa, but one that the world's best pathologists could not identify.

In his excitement, he set about explaining the pathology of the invaders who were assaulting my flesh. Then he explained the weapon to be used to stave off the invasion and administered it. And finally he crowned me with the honor of being the first American ever diagnosed in the U.S. with this disease. A disease which he could now put a name to - A.perstans, a rare form of Filariasis. Victoriously patting me on the shoulder, he left the room with honorable pride in his work, moving on to another medical challenge.

Though the news was great, it was also startlingly sudden and unexpected! Thoughts rolled through my mind like the dial on a slot machine. I had to pick them out one at a time. I was of course "on my knees" grateful that the disease was identified and a cure prescribed. I would again be able to take a hot shower without the hostile reaction from my back. And the festivities would end for the nematodes and our quasi-relationship would be dissolved. I will admit being a host to parasites was not my idea of a friendship, too one-sided, one might say. I came to detest the word nematode and will try to never have to write it again.

On the same knees where I was grateful for a cure, I rejoiced knowing I could return to Africa. As some might love a spouse, I loved Africa! Equally, I would avoid, for now, having to face that dreadfully lonely, dark void - both spiritually and socially - that I felt in America. Although I had recorded experiences in Africa that would be central to restoring my soul and outlook on life, I had yet to solidify these experiences into an organized set of values. That time was still to come.

I would need to spend several more days in the hospital to be monitored for any reaction to the drug hetrazan. Thankfully, there was none. But I would think how fortunate I was to be an American with this condition. I thought of the access I had to treatment, the money spent on plane tickets, great doctors, lab work, food and care. It was only a logical extension of this thought to think of what the Africans did not have. The care I was given seemed so easily provided and I was humbled and thankful. But I wished then and wish now that this treatment were available to Africa. There are so many, of all ages, who suffer and die from punishing diseases. They have no access to medical treatment that we just assume we have a "right" to.

I was so appreciative for the devotion given to my diagnosis and cure that I presented Dr. Dailey with my most prized possession, the bow and quiver of arrows given to me by the rain forest people, the Pygmies. He deserved it. His work allowed me to go back to Africa.

Lastly, I received a few moments of fame when put on display before a class of medical students. I was obliged for all that was done for me and so withheld my fee for this. I was discharged on February 16, 1979, just four days after being admitted. I then made immediate plans to return to Africa. I wished I could have found a way to take Dr. Dailey back with me.

Over time I would go on to suffer two episodes in Africa with another "unknown" that left me immobilized. I had two massive headaches so severe I had to lay perfectly flat for twenty-four hours. At first, I did not know how long the pain would last and was greatly relieved and thankful when it passed, as the slightest movement bordered on unbearable. The pain hit me instantly, lasted as if timed, for exactly twenty-four hours, disappeared immediately and I was fine. I was told it was dengue fever, but no blood test ever confirmed this. No longer was I just an outside, sympathetic observer; along with dysentery, and a painful, burning bite from a scorpion, I would become an experienced veteran of the suffering that I would continue to witness so much in Africa. Regardless, I loved being in that country.

*1971: Central Highlands of Vietnam.
Author's arrival – a box of hand grenades
serves as coffee table.*

*1972: Ben Hoa, Vietnam. Author one
year later – a different person.*

1976: Lebangy, Gabon Africa. School, which village children were attending when author first arrived with Peace Corps

1976: Lastoursville, Gabon Africa. New Peace Corps school on which author worked, constructed by Dick Steeper and Jeff Dennis.

1978: Lebangy Gabon. Village children – author's neighbors.

*1978: Lebangy Gabon. Another of author's neighbors
– a broom weaver selling his wares.*

1979: Gabon Africa. The main road leading to interior of Gabon.

1980: Mindif, Cameroun. Hospital lab – notice the hand crank centrifuge.

1981: Mindif, Cameroun. Lamido's cavalry (on horseback).

1981: Mindif, Cameroun. The Tooth of Mindif – a mountain climber's dream.

1981: Near Mindif, Cameroun. Villagers' conical roofed round houses with no corners and no evil spirits.

PART FOUR
RETURNING TO AFRICA,
THEN BACK TO AMERICA:
TRYING TO ESCAPE THE LAYERS
OF DECEPTION

"We must realize that all life is valuable and that we are united to all life. From this knowledge comes our spiritual relationship with the universe."
- Dr. Albert Schweitzer, *On the Edge of the Primeval Forest*

So many cultures understood our union with all life long ago but Americans have lost this belief in many areas. Is this because we consider ourselves such an advanced society, that we are so "much better than" other countries? The realization that America had lost so much of its connection to a spirit world and become so immersed in "self and materialism" was no place for a man like me whose experiences had left a devastated soul that could only be repaired in the spirit; that no material objects or money could help.

EGO MUST CHOOSE

CHAPTER TWENTY-THREE

Relieved and grateful from my experience with filarial, I left the hospital in Milwaukee. No sooner had I hit the outdoor air than it happened. The energy spent on that medical condition evaporated and flooded in from nowhere to replace the vacancy of spiritual darkness. Its onslaught set me to running again. I did not belong here; my mind begged to return to Africa and the peace and solitude that I knew awaited me there.

I had found a position with another organization for employment after my Peace Corps service. The work was to begin immediately if I could be medically cleared. I jumped at the job and once again the facade was restored, a new sanctuary to maintain its integrity for family, friends and society. I looked good to them, but I was desperate inside. I had to wait for visas, plane tickets, vaccinations, and normal travel preparations, but even this short period of two weeks in America was too long. I was extremely restless and filled with anxiety that screamed, "I want to leave here this minute!"

Unable to simply visit friends or family like a normal person home on leave, I headed for the Amtrak depot, and, not caring about a destination, grabbed a ticket on the next train out. I paced the marble floor, watching a clock that seemed bent on moving slowly for my personal torment, until boarding was finally announced. I felt I now understood the relief of someone being evacuated from a natural disaster. I moved quickly to the boarding platform and there, blazoned in large letters across an engine hissing fumes like a beagle anxious to get after a fox, I saw the words, Empire Builder. A fine name I thought. Strong, powerful. It would take me across Minnesota, the great northern plains and into Seattle, Washington. From there I would head north to Victoria, British Columbia, grab the Trans Canada Rail, and head back east across that country. "Just keep moving," is all I thought. Moving would occupy my thoughts and keep me from drifting to those tattered, old haunting memories of war.

Seated in the observation car, spending little time on sleep, I had to marvel at the vast beauty of the country. I was grateful for the opportunity to view the wonder of the plains, the rugged splendor of the northern Rocky Mountains, and the state of Washington. I was intrigued by the vastness of the landscape and curious about how many different people lived in this country; how diverse their circumstances in life must be. I was thrilled to view the almost unbelievable beauty of British Columbia, the Canadian Rockies at Banff and Calgary, and then on to the romance of Medicine Hat, Moose Jaw, Regina, Winnipeg, and all the intriguing names in between that beg one to stop and have a look around, smell the air, hear the voices, taste the food, and experience a tiny bit of what those folks call life. As I realized in Africa, to witness this world is to stand before it and marvel, to be reminded that I am such a small part of a life that is so much larger. And not just human life, but all of life. It was only in these extreme experiences that my mind was preoccupied enough to forget about the darkness of war. But as usual, the moment I stopped running, one person was always there to meet me - myself!

I left the train in Winnipeg very thankful for the experience. I hitchhiked by road back home to Wisconsin, and was now able to convert my thoughts to preparing for my return to Africa.

This filled my soul with joy and helped to avoid confrontation with the dark side. My new job was not in the tropical rain forest where I had been, but in the semi-arid land of north Cameroun, on the edge of the endless sands of the Sahara Desert. When flying out of Paris and approaching North Africa, I could not have guessed how vast the Sahara Desert is. By viewing a map I knew its size, but to fly over it the first time was quite another sense of just how magnificent the earth is and how tiny I am in its shadow.

For hours I watched an endless, lifeless moonscape of tan emptiness pass beneath the plane. But I knew better than that! *National Geographic* and my preparations told me that this place was anything but lifeless. I knew of the ancient camel routes crossing the Sahara, trading the salt of Mali for the gold of Egypt. I knew of the place an angry father always threatened to "knock you from here to" - Timbuktu - was actually a real place, and once the thriving intellectual and commercial center of western Africa. I knew that very old documents had been found to show mathematics centuries ahead of Western progress, and the astronomy of the planets established long before Copernicus came up with his calculations. I knew of the Touregs and the romantic elusiveness of this desert people, and I knew there was the desert array of other life. So, barren as it looked from the sky, I knew it was very much alive.

Finally landing in Yaoundé, Cameroun, my body said it was way past time to stretch and I was happy to accommodate it. I met project coordinators and Camerounian officials, then prepared to depart on the long, dusty trip by railroad and bush truck to the extreme, arid North, to the city of Mindif. I had not expected to be accompanied on the train by goats, chickens, and other live check-on luggage, but had learned long ago to adjust. Arriving in the world of the Arabs, nomadic herders, Moslems and animists, I began my new life as supervisor for the construction of the North Cameroun Agricultural and Livestock Project. As the only white guy and sole person from a Christian background, I felt – no, I knew – this was going to be interesting!

This culture was dramatically difference from life in the jungle and black Africa; here I faced a cold stalemate and fragile truce between cultures that was historic, going back to the times when Mohammed's armies swept out of the Middle East to capture North Africa and Southwest Europe. The retaliation had been the Christian Crusades led by the Knights Templar. In their competition for souls still continued, the two sides fought to a standstill, but the friction was everywhere in the air, and the competition for souls still continued, just as strongly. I felt too that if this truce melted away, I was sorely out numbered as the sole representative of the Christian world. Yet I had to stay in the realm of the human race and take no arrogant stance of judgment. I would need to live by simple rules of honesty and humanitarianism. I would be an observer without opinion. This would prove to be a great challenge considering the abundance of profound differences. I had a sense that I was acceptable because they were receiving a benefit from my work. Otherwise, I would have been in one way or another chased away from there.

While courtesy required that I introduce myself to the Lamido, the traditional leader of Mindif, curiosity made the requirements an adventure. Walking the dry, dusty streets I found my way through the high, mud walled labyrinth of neighborhoods, passing men in traditional Arab dress who watched me pass with frigid, uninviting stares. As I passed each, I could feel his eyes added to the collection of others that kept me fixed in their sights. Asking directions brought only the point of a hand, never a word. Again I felt that uneasy truce and collision of cultures that was centuries in the making. And what century? I had the number 638 in my head. I knew if I subtracted that number from whatever year the Western calendar was on, I'd be close to the year of the Moslem calendar. So, I was now in the year 1342!

Arriving at the opening to the Lamido's walled compound,

I was met by two guards armed with old bolt-action rifles. A cold nod of the head passed me through and I found myself in the midst of a tiny militia of armed men, the Lamido's personal guards. No one could get to this man without a stiff battle. Escorted across the grounds I was overwhelmed with excitement. Entering the main building, expecting to find royalty and riches, I was stunned when led into a room and introduced to an old, white-haired man sitting on his bed. By Arab style dress I could not tell if he was in traditional dress or his white pajamas. He did not get up, only looked in my direction, squinting through tiny slits that made me wonder if he was blind. The loaded military .45-caliber pistol at his side said he was not. Through his interpreter I introduced myself and explained my purpose there. The meeting was short and business like.

I would have several of these meetings during my stay in Mindif and feel sad that our history would never allow the conversations to wander away from business to a friendly exchange about life in our different cultures. It did not escape me that in Africa the traditional leaders hold the real power over the people; the modern administrative government was present to interact with the outside world but held little power over the day-to-day lives of the population. This Lamido was no different, as I would later learn. A lover of black magic and fetishes, he controlled the people with a brutal hand. I would leave Mindif only a few years before the town would slip into ruinous dark times for individual rights, security and peace. As with so many dictators, his terror and oppression of his own people for his benefit was cowardly; maybe this explained the .45-caliber pistol at his side.

Unlike the accepting cultures of black Africa, I sensed the purposefulness of those powerful people, deeply and singularly loyal to their culture and religion. And I had no doubt that in their historic conflicts with the Christian world, they had been formidable opponents. Where in Gabon I was greeted openly and encouraged to "find a woman"; where I had been invited to all social activities and ceremonies; where I was invited into homes for dinner; where neighbors stopped by regularly and I was just another villager absorbed into the culture, the total opposite was true here. Not once in the year and a half that I lived there was I invited to participate in the culture. Not one visitor came to my house nor was I invited to anyone's. Interaction with women (if they could be seen) would have been an invitation to die; children would not come near as the curious little neighbors had in Gabon.

Though polite and formal where work was concerned, all other interactions were frosty, at best. There was little, if any, open, curious conversation between two cultures. I did have the suspicion that if I had declared a desire to become a Moslem, the gates to the world would have opened, and I would have been received and absorbed into the culture heartily. It was my representation of the Christian world that formed the wall between us.

But organized religion had severely failed me at war, and was not even a remote desire now. Yet life remained fascinating for I could find deep intrigue in observing the culture and spend endless hours studying the amazing wildlife of this arid land.

I traveled outside of Mindif to visit the remote cultures of the Kurdish people. These were animists – the very name Kurd, given to them by the Moslem Fulani, means pagan. And as were Christians, the Kurds were severely discriminated against by the Moslems; this was open and obvious. The Kurds lived in round mud houses with conical roofs, whereas the Fulani lived in rectangular houses surrounded by tall mud walls forming compounds like hives, which were accessible by narrow, dark walkways. The Kurdish people were subsistence growers of millet, cotton, maize and groundnuts, and they were to benefit from the project we were building. The goal was to help improve crop quality and output. From what I saw, this was a much-needed service for I could not imagine how anything grew in that dry, rocky soil.

The other aspect of the North Cameroun Agriculture and Livestock Project was to improve the health of livestock, and develop better grazing methods that would prevent overgrazing and loss of the meager topsoil available to sustain grasses. This part of the project concerned the nomadic herders and the Fulani cattle owners. I was proud to participate in this project for the objectives were sound and desperately needed.

In my experience as an observer and through rare conversations with non-Moslems living in Maroua, the capital of the Far North Province of Cameroun, which was about a half hour drive away, I learned something very important regarding the rules of man in creating organized societies, and the societies' reaction to those rules. This was the topic of male-female sexual interaction. Whether spoken of, thought of, or acted upon, there is no doubt that sex is one of the most pervasive, fundamental and powerful interactions of the human race. That is understood, but what impresses me is the different attitude, different cultures give this interaction. That nature prepared men and women for this at the same age world-wide is one thing - what humans have added as controls is quite another.

In Gabon, sex was open and expected as soon as nature made the person ready. There were no constraints, no shame, no laws; childbirth was normal at thirteen, fourteen or fifteen years of age. The Gabon women had been doing this forever and childbirth at these ages was simply normal. Males and females interacted openly and freely. Not to engage in sex was the unusual situation. In contrast, in the Moslem world of North Cameroun, the control of women was oppressive and brutal. Women were not allowed in public alone, never looked a man in the eyes, never engaged a man in conversation, and were always clothed from foot to head. To stray from these rules set down by men would earn severe beatings. The women were kept hidden behind the mud walls of their compounds. All of these were means of controlling the normal sexual desires of a woman to be saved for the man who claimed ownership of her. A woman caught in a sexual affair literally put her life at risk. And the stories of physical mutilation to prevent a young girl from being precocious and sexy are true.

I thought of the rules set out in American society for sex. Sex is everywhere - present and powerful as anywhere in the world. But we override nature and set an age where sexual interaction for a woman should begin. For women who break this rule a stigma is attached that can ruin a reputation for life. The penalty for a man or woman engaging in consensual sex with a person younger than the required age can be years in prison and a permanent record as a felonious sexual offender. This preoccupation with sex seems to occupy an enormous amount of human energy and time. It is not the topic that impresses me, but the world's different societal setting of rules and regulations. It was at war that the rules set out by American society had failed me, but these were rules by our society and not rules universal to all human thought and activity. I felt as though many regulations were for suckers who believed them and could be controlled by their fallacy.

But deeper thought showed me why societies exist and that rules had to be established for the general good and benefit of its members. In all of the societies that I experienced, I saw good and beautiful, evil and bad. It no longer seemed important to angrily confront the rules that had failed me as if they had been designed for that purpose; this was purely foolish thinking. It seemed more logical to realize that spectacle and majesty of life was far beyond my comprehension. But I could still be amazed, respect, and honor it. I knew that my ego was insignificant on its own; that I must surrender a part of my ego to the larger ego of all life. And in being a part of that ego of all life I had a choice: be part of making it better, be part of making it worse or, as my ma would say, "Heaven forbid," be part of doing nothing at all.

And so, on completing my work in Cameroun and preparing to return home, I began reflecting on life there. I remembered the people digging a wide hole 5 ft. deep into a dry riverbed desperately looking for water. I remembered the women who came to the water hole to do laundry just after stray cattle had spent time wallowing around and urinating in it. Later the women came with clay pots to collect that same water for cooking and drinking. I thought of my own participation in building very modern homes, a veterinary clinic, office buildings; all complete with plumbing, electricity from a generator, tiled showers, and washers and dryers – structures to be proud of in most American cities. I thought of how the floor plans were rectangular and American-style since American money had supplied them. That no one asked the African people who were to use those buildings why, as animists, they lived in round houses. Then to find out on completion of the project that those folks would not go into the buildings because evil spirits live in corners. There was no choice but to laugh at our own folly.

And I will never forget the nights spent sitting on top of a granite outcrop staring in awe at an ocean of stars so brilliantly clear and in numbers an astronomer would not believe and again realize how tiny I was in this spectacular place. And I would understand how these people in and near the Sahara Desert - who spend half their lives in the hours of darkness gazing into this wonderment - were the great navigators of the earth, using the night sky as their map. How in touch with the physical world are these people!

ASSAULT ON THE SOUL

CHAPTER TWENTY-FOUR

Back home in America, a new war was beginning. Unlike the war in Asia, this new war would have no machine guns, no grenades, no helicopters, no medics, no artillery, no companions to share the fears, no re-supply and no field radios to call for help. The weapons of this new war would be alcohol, cigarettes, overeating, and bulimia. I was fighting the losing battle for the fortification and defense of my facade. This new war would rage on for over twenty-five years and be fought on the battlefield of my mind.

Back in the US, PTSD began its open assault on me. I did not fit in at home: I felt alienated and was again faced with a world of materialism and things that would not balance the agony of my mind. Again I was wrapped in a world I could not figure out, a mind overloaded with too many events, and the inability to solve them out one by one. So my mind was at a standstill. It could absorb no more nor could it resolve issues to make room for new thoughts. I was just barely getting by.

The next several years would be spent kicking around my hometown. I was listless, unmotivated, and my brain seemed waterlogged. I was going absolutely nowhere, physically, mentally, and of course, spiritually. Behind the facade once again was a storage place for all that was dark and evil. I was filled with deep hatred, shame, and anger, and all of my energies went to keeping them in their container. Nothing came out and nothing good went in. It was like all the information for an evil weapon had been given to the wrong person. I had the information, but had no idea how to use it. It was far too complicated for my bewildered mind to comprehend.

Looking back, I now understand why an eighteen-year-old is the perfect candidate for the military. For some ungodly reason a kid at that age is reliable, will become part of the "team," will be enticed to become courageous, and will charge into battle thinking he is doing the honorable thing. At that age you swallow everything you are told and perform at the expected level because no eighteen to twenty-year-old wants to be labeled a coward. That label would be a fate worse than death. Those who have experienced tremendous fear know its shame, but to be unable to act under pressure and be labeled a coward is not acceptable; you'd rather be dead. These thoughts are drilled into the mind of a young person. The military has the upper hand, and the leaders know it. I'd heard of some men claiming to be war veterans without having served. If they only knew the price paid to be called a war veteran, they would never envy it nor pretend to be one.

Society needs to think of its military as this "pure clean assembly of men and women" who could not possibly abuse prisoners, shoot their own soldiers, or become mentally traumatized. Society needs to believe that its military is honorable, courageous, and fights within the rules for a clean, clear victory. Our society wants one thing – to be secure at home. We mask over many problems to have that security, and war veterans are a big part of it. They must return heroic and unaffected by the experience. It just doesn't work that way.

In recent wars such as Somalia and Bosnia, society expected to engage in war with very few casualties. What do we do now that casualties are high? Will the need to feel secure at home become the goal at all costs? When pushed to real warfare for the sake of survival, the Geneva Convention will go out the window. It was written to ease the guilt of those at home. The intellectuals who support the Geneva Convention have not experienced war. When survival is the object, WAR HAS NO RULES! Why do you think we have atomic weapons? Do those fit the Geneva Convention?

It stuns me when I read in the news that a police officer who shoots a suspect at a crime scene, is put on leave and provided psychological counseling. When tragedies strike in a school - as many have recently – the entire school is flooded with ministers and psychologists to aid the students, parents and teachers. Many who have not even witnessed the crime are affected because it happened in their world. Why in God's name would anyone expect that an eighteen-year-old can go into the military, be trained for three months, go off to see people blown to pieces before their eyes, experience the incredible carnage of war, witness civilians running around on fire with napalm glued to their bodies, watch people pinned to trees with a flachette round from artillery that fires thousands of tiny little metal arrows, and suffer from no repercussions whatsoever? These young men and women see people killed by heavy machine gun fire, bodies torn to shreds, the screaming insanity during battle and the pain of the wounded and the cries for one's mother. They are in a state of mental alertness twenty-four hours a day, every day for months, just desperately hoping for their own salvation from the insanity. Then to come home and be expected to be normal and not need psychological help is an insane concept. But society must have security without guilt. After all, that is what an Army is supposed to do and the personal devastation is left to the warriors

Remember, we are now living in a society where you can go to jail for abusing an animal. Society seeks to purify itself of acts that are repulsive, yet at the same time creates weapons that cause inconceivable devastation to the life of others in countries who might threaten our safety or have what we want. So, as society abhors violence inside its own boundaries and moves to purify its conscience, we create citizens who have little, if any, experience with death. As the weapons of war become more devastating, PTSD is going to become more severe.

Imagine you are given a sentence of twelve months for having committed no offense, and are sent to live on a large island, which you cannot leave until those twelve months have passed. Let's have two teams, say of five guys each. Your team of five is in military dress and the other team dresses as typical islanders. The objective is to kill the five men on the other team. You search them out as they search you out to kill you with whatever weapons or booby traps they choose. Now add an unknown number of native islanders who go about their normal activities, but you are not sure which are legitimate workers and which are out to kill you! You cannot be sure if the legitimate islanders are helping the other side. You know only that you have to spend twelve months trying to find the other team and kill them before they kill you!

You have weapons and ammunition, food and a bed roll; you must sleep on the ground and you can strike at or be struck at any time of day or night; you can be killed any second, and you wonder why you have been given this insane sentence. You cannot communicate with family or friends except by mail and you realize there is a strong possibility you will never see wife, kids, husband or friends again.

I remember having a conversation in the jungle of Vietnam with two friends in which we discussed how we did not want to be killed. One said, "Not shot in the heart." The other said, "Not in the 'masculines.'" We finally agreed that the worst way to be killed would to be shot in the face, our logic being that the face is how we are identified and to die this way would be a total and complete annihilation of self. Now keep in mind, we were only twenty-years-old, but imagine even having to have that conversation at that young age! We should have been dating, planning careers, and spending time with our friends and families. Death should not have been even remotely in our minds, yet death was everywhere in our thoughts, an everyday reality.

So, now I was back home in the America. Having served my time in the Peace Corps and worked for the United States Agency for International Development, I was far from the safe haven and good works of Africa. Back home, the facade I used to cover my pain had nothing to reinforce its image. College had failed, my marriage had failed, and yet I could not expose the destruction behind the facade even to myself.

ROAMING DARKNESS, COMPASSIONATE SUICIDE

CHAPTER TWENTY-FIVE

I had no direction professionally and no real ambition socially unless alcohol was involved, and so I began a life of just getting by. Alcohol was a friend, and to stay near that friend I took a job bartending at a local restaurant. Living completely in a facade is a huge lie. I could joke and laugh in the facade but no one got beyond that, including female relationships. The facade was so sophisticated it could actually sustain a relationship for a time. But the cold loneliness of my soul was a torment no one could see.

My first relationship fueled by alcohol was easy the first couple of years. My facade held up well, as did the woman's. But when alcohol is all a relationship has, misery and loneliness are the inevitable result. And when you are – as I was – already shattered inside, you choose to stay in the misery of the relationship, as I did for three additional years. It is truly amazing how I could live behind a facade containing such emptiness and loneliness, but I had no place to run, mentally or spiritually; my head was too full of images of war, and spiritually I felt bankrupt. I have no complaint against the woman. She also had to deal with her own demons. After the thrill of the first year had passed we were sustained by alcohol and superficial but meaningless adventures.

After a while, I left the bartending job to start my own remodeling business. My soul was in such desperate need for repair that I could only survive. There was no dream of becoming a great builder, no dream of owning a great house or car. It looked like a road to success, but I set my own hours and alcohol claimed a lot of them. If I were employed, I would have been unemployed very quickly for poor attendance. I drank any day I chose and just hired sub-contractors to do the work. It was ideal for me. I was the salesman, made sure the job site had materials, and then I could hide in my misery at home. No relationship could have saved me. I was hoping for that but found it just didn't work. Nobody could understand, nor make sense out of what I could not make sense of myself. The relationship soured, failed, and was over. I was happy to see the end of the facade of companionship which had nothing like good health, not to mention love, to give.

So I began my years of wandering and living with brothers and sisters, lost in a cloud, drinking nights and taking small jobs just to keep in cigarettes and booze and gas for the truck. I deeply believe that had it not been for my five sisters and four brothers, I would have been destitute on the streets and very likely dead from one cause or another.

At first, I drifted to an older sister's home. She and her family took me in and I was regarded with love and affection. I continued to just get by, do whatever it took to make a few bucks to keep some minute sense of respect and afford the necessary materials for my habits. My cars were usually the type that an automatic car wash would reject because the car body and was more rust than metal. But these cars got me to the bar. I was in deep emotional pain that I could share with no one. The facade was losing its phony luster and I just couldn't figure out what was wrong. Why couldn't I get my life together? I was barely hanging on. I tried exercise but was too depressed to keep at it. I tried yoga and it helped but I was not mentally capable of

Michael S. Orban

the routine. I tried biofeedback-breathing techniques and got the same results as yoga. Intellectually I knew what to do to improve my physical and mental health but some deep, dark internal counterforce kept me from it. Alcohol dulled everything and protected my facade from attack.

My youngest brother, Tom, was living in California when the disastrous 1989 earthquake hit San Francisco. He and his family were at the World Series when it hit. They were terribly frightened and it took them many extra hours to get to their home in Monterey. He and his wife and first-born son decided to trade earthquakes for hurricanes and moved back to Naples, Florida, his wife's hometown, nearer to family. His wife and baby flew to Florida and my brother asked me to help him load his rental truck and drive with him from California to Florida. I jumped at the chance because even this slight adventure would help the facade and give me credibility. I ended up staying with him and his family for several years; no lack of alcohol, no rent, food was provided and I worked as a painter for Tom's painting company. Again, had this opportunity not arisen, I'd have been on the streets.

All this time I was just barely holding the facade together. I felt no shame living with family when I clearly should have. I just could not get relief from the savagery of the parts behind the facade. That area of my soul frightened me. I had no real spiritual values, no social connections. I was isolated in my own world and its pains. No one could understand, because I could not explain. They understood that I was just "not the same as before the war" but did not know why. They saved my life with their generosity and love.

After two years, I began feeling really out of place and ready for a change to replenish the facade. I returned to my older sister's home in Wisconsin where once again they were kind and generous, and never charged me for rent or food. Just think how cleaned out a person must be mentally and spiritually to not recognize that this was not appropriate for a single forty-two-year-old! It just did not register with me as wrong. I was a man on the ropes struggling not to hit the mat. During these years, I had no dates and was angry that I was in no condition to even have a companion. I would not know the joy of having my own family, or the joy of a companion to share my inner secrets because I could not face them myself.

I know in writing this down that it seems redundant to repeat again and again that I could not face what lay behind the facade, but that is how empty, scared and lonely I was. That is how intense those experiences were and how frightened I was to face them. I had come to feel comfortable being shattered. Restoring myself was incomprehensible. I had no idea that a new reality would have to replace the old, and what knowledge did I have to rebuild that soul? None! I would have to live that shattered life.

I remember driving down the street in one of my rusty old cars during rush hour. I was crying outright, banging my hands on the steering wheel and begging out loud to know why I was so different. Why couldn't I be like everyone else? Why did they have goals and nice cars, jobs, enjoy life and I was broken down with no motivation or answers for my own agony? Tears would come many times over the years and for the same desperate questions: What's wrong with me? Why can't I fit in?

Later when I was working small remodeling jobs to maintain my drinking habit and gas for any car, I was introduced to a female bar owner. It would turn out to be an absurd relationship; two people who have drinking problems are the perfect combination for the production of misery. This relationship was no different than the one before because again I was clinging to anyone and anything (especially alcohol) to keep from giving up – just to have something and someone. The first couple of months were the typical passion of a new relationship, but when the newness wore off and our facades bumped into one another, the relationship began failing tremendously. But, as people do when emotionally on the ropes, I stayed in that one for two years. I was too afraid to be alone, afraid not to have someone. No matter how miserable I was in the relationship, it felt more normal than being alone.

When the relationship could take no more, I found myself alone again with my façade, which was now turning against me in a painful way. The cover-up was not working any more. My family knew that I was having big trouble. As is the case, alcohol is a friend until it turns against you. And it did! And at the same time the pressure cooker of my mind was ready to explode. Everything failed me in some sort of strange, systemic irony. I was drinking a bottle of whisky a day and staying secluded in my little 8' x 10' bedroom at my younger sister's home. I lived there pretty much free of charge; I just had to buy my own cigarettes, booze, and gas for the excuse of a car that was still attached to the four wheels in the driveway. Alcohol had now become my enemy. It changed my logic, depressed me severely. It no longer brought any relief, not even phony laughter. It was now revealing the lies of my facade desperately trying to fool the world and pretend that I was respectable. People could see right through me. I was a drunk and drunken most of the time, but I thought I was under control and no one could tell I was drinking. Alcohol fools people that way. I was painfully lonely and sad, way out of touch with any emotions.

I was standing in the living room of my younger sister's flat, drunk in the afternoon, when the landlord called to say if the rent wasn't paid, we'd have to move. By now my thinking was so distorted it didn't seem to matter and I thought, "So what if I end up on the streets?" When alcohol turns against you, you find yourself drinking all day – 3:00 pm, 11:00 pm, 2:00 am – whenever your body demands, and I mean demands alcohol. Not in ten minutes, not in an hour, but now! That is a very dangerous time and you can literally kill yourself. But that didn't register. Who really cared anyway?

The next day I was again in my isolation (I left only to buy booze and cigarettes) standing in the living room when I swear to the mountaintops that the second option I had thought of earlier appeared before me. I stared suicide right in the eyes. The idea was so solid it was a physical being I could reach out and touch. Then suicide, presented its options: Either kill yourself or face what is behind the facade. I don't know where the courage came from but I decided that no matter what was behind the facade, however incomprehensible, no matter how little confidence I had in believing that I could handle what was there, the choice was clear. I could either become willing to face the truth inside or die right then.

As eerie as it may sound, I wasn't really afraid of suicide. I had a sense of strength and anger within the façade and I wasn't giving in. The facade itself was now my enemy and I knew without a doubt that I could not let it win. I made a decision then and there that I would turn and face it and do whatever I had to do to resolve those issues buried for the past twenty-four years. And if I did drop off into some form of insanity when I faced the truth, so be it. But I would at least stick around long enough to confront the facade and the tatters and shreds that lay behind it. I knew it would take time, maybe years, to solve those pains. I was single, had no kids and nothing to lose; I would face my demons on my own.

PART FIVE
REMOVING THE FACADE: FACING THE TRUTH OF DARKNESS

A VET'S POEM

Can those boys you send to war
When after having done that chore
Come home to you in khakis pressed
And medals dripping from their chests
Return, as you would hope to see
The men you now want them to be
Look past the decorated chest
Deep into eyes that tell the rest
Don't be afraid to take their hand
And though you may not understand
Listen as their souls pour out
Of all the horrors that came about

When deep in combat drenched in fear
They saw their boyhood disappear
Replaced now with another view
Of what a human being can do
Where all the rules he learned before
Do not exist there any more
Of fears and death and agony
That he could not be trained to see
All wretched as he comes to know
His soul was dealt a heavy blow
And knowing now what humans are
Must try to heal a deadly scar

So listen when he reaches out
To tell you what it's all about
Listen hard and try to feel
It's what must be if he should heal
Be thankful too that he was blessed
To have come home with all the rest
For there were others, once your boys
Who will never hear another noise
And when you hear those others roar
That there must be another war
Think long and hard and contemplate
If you would choose war as your fate

Michael S. Orban

THE ENEMY UNVEILED

CHAPTER TWENTY-SIX

It was obvious the facade I had created to convince the world that I was fine was crumbling. It had become a worn out, tattered rag of a show. The energy needed to maintain the facade was gone, and the ache of the suffering self behind the facade was demanding serious attention. Caring what the world thought about me had produced no measurable amount of happiness, so maintaining the facade was an empty goal. Besides, it didn't really matter what the world thought because the facade was a lie anyway. I needed to face the truth inside me, for me.

And so I entered the world of psychiatrists and psychologists. I dragged the tatters of my soul around, exposing them first to one doctor, then another. My decision to get professional help was a desperate move to obtain relief from unbearable mental and spiritual suffering. I genuinely thought these folks would wave a magic wand and all would be happiness again. I had the belief that this was the power they held. I just needed to turn myself over and let them get about the healing.

Four psychiatrists, psychologists, lots of money and years with no change in symptoms, I thought it wise to adjust my thinking. It was an education in itself as I learned these genuinely concerned professionals have no magical potions, nor do they hand out magical powers or instant relief of symptoms. Each doctor has his or her own personal approach and the doctor and patient need to be compatible.

I realized that taking antidepressants was not a good choice for me, but I cannot say they are not right for others. I also learned that these people were not there to guide my life, but to offer an opportunity for me to take control of my own life, and help the sufferer achieve this goal. But most significantly, I learned that whatever it was that I suffered from did not appear in their textbooks. Please note, I am not complaining I had such an incredible condition that I was unique and special. This was the 1980s and though I did mention to each doctor that I was a combat veteran of the Vietnam War, none of them ever brought up the subject again. They had not heard of PTSD in those days. Things are different now. Spending time with one doctor then the other, reminiscing about my relationship with my parents, siblings and past youthful happiness, was not what I needed.

I became more of a friend with two of these folks and actually used my discount to purchase building materials for their home projects. They seemed to think that I might find the answers in written tests and came up with no end of these to torment me. Minneapolis tests – or something of the sort – took hours and yielded the enlightening result that I had no particular professional aim. A quick review of remarks from the very first meeting would have shown this too. I was not impressed that those hours-long tests came up with the same result, but I was impressed in being separated from more money. When the result of yet another test informed all parties that my IQ was around 150, I sensed I should have been filled with pride when told this qualified me to belong to Mensa. Agitated and disappointed, I had three immediate thoughts: I could not be that intelligent because I had no idea what Mensa meant. Joining a club at the moment sparked no enthusiasm in me, I was trying to recover from the last one I was invited to join, and had come to have a cold suspicion of these things. Secondly, I was impressed by the detail that I had never received a more useless piece of information in my life! (I got the mental picture of being caught in the deadly vortex of a mid-western tornado and was expected to be thrilled when given a badminton racket.) And third, another written test had shifted more cash away from my pile with nothing in the way of benefit to replace it.

I must mention that these were all well positioned professionals, not psychiatrists and psychologists with offices in coffee shops or on park benches. The topic of the war was never approached because these folks kept the conversation in the realm of their education and experience, and they did not understand war. My sessions seemed as though I was a house on fire with all its occupants inside, and they were focused on making repairs to my car because that is what they knew. So, after years, I finally demanded: "Do you think this has anything to do with my being a war veteran?" Conversation stopped cold; the house fire was faced. Taking the phone, the doctor made a call to the Veterans Hospital. I was immediately referred to be tested for POST TRAUMATIC STRESS DISORDER. Neither the doctor nor I had ever heard the term. This was now the early 1990s.

While I speak badly of those years, I want to be clear that these were wonderful, caring professionals. PTSD was simply not widely known. I really did become friends with two of these doctors and still respect them. Today the entire worlds of psychiatry and psychology have made huge advances on the topic and once identified, these great professionals have devoted much to understanding the condition. And it must be understood that in the early 1970s, while I was receiving counseling through the Veterans Administration, they were not aware of PTSD either, but now give tremendous attention and help for it. The help is there for anyone who needs to resolve issues and improve the quality of his or her life and the lives of their loved ones. So, go get it!

I was diagnosed with PTSD in 1992. It would be a couple of years yet before I was aware of an active therapy program.

INDOMITABLE SPIRIT

CHAPTER TWENTY-SEVEN

Now understanding that PTSD was real and I was not alone in this experience, I began to attack it by researching history. I found that many combat veterans from past wars had had this response, but kept it hidden as I had. I listened to stories of wives and family members whose veterans had suffered alone pacing floors in the middle of the night, and experiencing bouts with alcohol and depression, and been awakened by nightmares many years after returning from their wars.

I met a Korean War veteran who had been a combat medic in charge of twelve other medics. He was the only one to return home. I listened to his stories of alcohol abuse, losing his job, and the depression that kept him in therapy for fifty years after his military duty. When I began speaking publicly of this, a whole world of people began to tell me of their veterans who had suffered in the quiet secrecy of family and home. The suffering was no different from war to war. And more importantly, these veterans were those who had honorably and courageously served their country as it had asked. These were not whiners and crybabies who had avoided that task. And I knew so many veterans of the Vietnam War who had spent their time honorably serving their country, and then suffering alone on their return. I read that

Audie Murphy, the great hero of World War II, had warned to watch out for post traumatic stress during the Vietnam War in the 1960s, twenty years after his experiences.

History informed me that Charlemagne had wept openly for days on the battlefields where his friends had died. Other terms for PTSD like combat fatigue and shell shock are all over history, if one chooses to look for them. And of course, my own high school friend had taken his life after war. He was a veteran of the battle on Firebase Maryann in 1971 - a very bloody battle, recorded as one of the bloodiest in the previous four years of the Vietnam War. Reading and listening to these stories, filled me with the same anger and compassion as when I hear an American say, "I know a Vietnam veteran, and man, is he messed up."

For anyone to go off to war and come home unaffected by that experience, well now, that would be the scary person! I used to be glad that Americans do not understand war and the resulting issues of veterans. That they do not understand the war experience meant the soldiers had done their job. The only way for citizens of America to understand the veteran would be for war to come to our country. I don't believe any veteran would want that just so his/her experience could be understood. Nor can I, as a veteran, expect to receive understanding from family or friends, or even look in that direction unless I honestly want them to have experienced war so they could understand; this makes no sense. I should be proud and happy in my soul that they cannot understand war and leave it at that. But I am concerned that this statement about "messed up vets" is so widely known that many veterans will hide deeper behind the facade to avoid that label rather than doing everything to make their lives and those of their families the happiest possible.

As I delved deeper into the darkness behind my façade, it no longer mattered to me what the world thought as much as what I thought. And although I was now aware of the term Post Traumatic Stress, I also realized this is just a clinical name. It was more important for me to recognize that war causes severe changes and that I could take actions to understand those changes and myself. It had been over twenty years since my return from war and putting up a facade for others had brought neither relief nor rewards. The answer had to be somewhere else.

Here was the huge issue for me. Why was it that I didn't feel these reactions to war during my years in Africa? Where'd the reactions go? Why in Africa was I so happy in spirit, free to laugh, without nightmares, anxiety, twitching muscles and grinding teeth? Where had the rage and temper gone? Why did I sleep so deeply on a straw bed in a mud house deep in the jungles of Africa, in a culture so dramatically different from my own? As notably, how and why did those feelings resurface so devastatingly the moment I returned to America? Where had those feelings been? It had to be something inside of me that controlled the response. Or, it had to be something about America that did not exist in Africa that elicited this response. In remembering the years spent in Africa and how the people and cultures fit so beautifully into nature, I felt refreshed in spirit. I was startled to hear birds singing again. At home in America, I no longer heard those songs nor noticed the beauty of life; I had stopped marveling at it.

I knew by being honest with myself that I could identify some of the stronger issues and so I began to write about them. Writing became a means of isolating and understanding individual ideas out of my swirl of thoughts. I needed no prodding to recognize my vicious hatred of the American government and politicians in it during my time in Vietnam. That American soldiers were so casually treated as inanimate objects by those leaders in a pathetic inability to conduct a war, and the actual lives lost, left a blinding rage in me that was hard to get past. Many Americans cannot understand this, but when it is your very life being given away with no more regard than throwing away a banana peel, your opinion changes. This also had the effect of shattering my belief in the concept of countrymen. These were the acts of cowards. Melting away with that belief were my childhood lessons of "respect your elders." This idea of blind belief in and respect for elders evaporated after I experienced what some were capable of.

During this time I was reading Mark Twain's hilarious short stories. These stories helped temper and even remove some of the anger. Stories like "On Running for Governor" and "Cannibalism in the Cars" made me howl with laughter at the buffoonery of politicians. Moreover, Twain's writings showed me that politicians had been buffoons for centuries and were not just an aberration during my era. I had to accept this as a reality of the human condition and not something directed at me. Mark Twain's laughter at the human race and himself, as in his tale, "A True Story" showed me I had more to be grateful for than many who have gone before me. His writings helped me learn to laugh again, and most importantly, at myself. I understood that I had held the human race and its rules and regulations to standards that they never could meet.

I reflected again on religion, one of the most severe conflicts of my life. I did not know then, nor do I understand now, how a religion can take its most fundamentally sacred rules and at the same time align itself with an organization whose very purpose is to break those sacred rules. This conflict and my refusal to accept this reasoning had left a dark spiritual void. But I have since read *Beyond Belief: The Secret Gospel of Thomas* by Elaine Pagels, professor and theologian at Princeton University. The book that shows the "Gospel of Thomas" which courageously declares that we can seek to know God directly without dependence on an organized church. I have seen the beautiful religion of the Pygmies and their direct interaction with God and the jungle, their cathedral. I have seen other religions in the world and have come to believe, as the Pygmies, that everywhere we go, we are in church and interacting with God. Also, I have learned to not judge any religion, or blame any religion for failing me, but realized that we are diverse in our relationships with God. I must pay attention to the relationship I develop with God as my soul seeks to know its truth. In this

I have found enormous freedom from fear, and my soul is calm and grateful.

I searched inside myself to understand the rage at countrymen who, by their actions, had been directly responsible for the opposing forces taking new enthusiasm to kill American soldiers. This was not anger like, "You dented my new car!" Rather this was a blinding rage at those who could create deadly results for those of us - their countrymen whose lives were directly at risk - while they avoided the chaos they created by hiding in the safety of America. I extended this rage to reporters who sought notoriety by using their position to deeply defame the American soldier by characterizing only the horrible events. In reality there was no greater occurrence of these events in the military than in the general population of America. And most deeply, I was angered at the American population that did little, if anything, to stand up for us, their countrymen, and recognize the enormous difference between the obligations of the military and the politicians who send an Army to war. At twenty-one years of age, I was profoundly shocked by all of this and felt there was no honor in America.

The concept that "people don't go to war, nations do" seemed a huge lie. It felt more like a military goes to war and its country turns against it. If a president came into office and brought along his own loyal, paid for military, I could understand the retaliation. But the military is loyal to their country and responds to the person that country elects as president, therefore it is that country that is responsible for that president's activities. But years of traveling the world have shown me that this is the reality of the human race. Perhaps I was so deeply angered because life was not what I had expected. I began to sense that it was no longer the object of my anger that was important, but the fact that I was holding that anger inside me, regardless of the reasons. It was the anger itself that I had come to despise. It was the anger that became fatiguing, making me miserable, and preventing me from leaving those experiences behind and moving on. I had been trapped in the void of spiritual darkness but now saw this was by choice and it would be my choice to either stay there or leave. I believed that by holding the anger I was assuming the role of judge. I was judging by anger because life had not evolved, as I had wanted. A great step in my life was to give up the role of judge and let the anger go. Anger is a horrible burden and can be completely debilitating. To stop holding it inside is a choice one eventually has to make to grow spiritually. Whether one acts on the anger or lets it go then it becomes the choice.

Young war veterans have often expressed that they came home from war feeling like old men. I have thought of this and watched men actually grow older in society. It is generally a gentle transition where change comes slowly over the years and the issues of life come one at a time. Returning from the experiences of war can feel more like the instantaneous and cataclysmic failure of the beliefs that explain life. With a belief system that has failed, the darkness of a frightening spiritual void absorbs you; a spiritual void where the intellectual memories of life before war are used to develop a facade to hide this spiritual darkness. To rebuild a belief system that makes sense of life is not easy, but this is essential for getting out from behind the facade and facing the truth of the darkness.

NOW I SEE IT!!!!

CHAPTER TWENTY-EIGHT

By experiencing different cultures, religions and political systems I came to understand why societies were organized. I could see that men set out the rules and regulations for societies and these rules differed dramatically from society to society. I also realized that the American rules and regulations I grew up with were quite solid while living within that society. However, when sent out of that society, as I was to engage in war, these social rules no longer applied. I entered a world with a different set of rules.

The extreme intensity of this new world was centered on survival – a world where the stress of knowing that life could end in an insanely brutal and gruesome way was almost unbearable. Having to make sense of this new world created a new reality where death was the constant focus and staying alive was the only goal. It is my belief that the experience of being in this new world formed the deep friendships of which some veterans speak. They face death in a world outside their earlier reality; they bond with others who are living in the same desperate situation. But maybe these are not two different realities but one is an extension of the other. It is just one that not all experience. Maybe we should not try too hard to forget but and choose to know the beauty of life and fearlessly live it.

Over and over Africa showed me survival of the human animal. From young children to the elderly, this instinct to survive was evident. Facing serpent or gorilla, elephant or vicious monkeys, the reaction to survive was there. This is exactly what we did at war; we used an instinct not given by the rules of man but by a higher source, nature. In a situation where survival is paramount, there should be no shame in surviving; it is a natural reaction.

Realizing there may be plenty of anger in having been put in a situation to use that survival instinct, there comes also certain disgust and anger in seeing what members of the human race can do to one another. One can create a sense of not wanting to belong to the only club whose membership cannot be canceled - the membership in the human race. But it is more important to realize that this is real, this is what humans do, not just at war but also in society in general. It seems more important for me not to be concerned with what others believe, not to live behind a dishonest mask, but believe in what I have seen and do this without fear. I cannot pretend that certain experiences did not happen and deny them. I must not be afraid to acknowledge these truths. So realizing that the rules people develop for societies are general guidelines to prevent chaos, it seems absolutely foolish to spend any time standing in anger against those rules, or that society, simply because they failed at war.

Coming out of the world of war and its reality and re-entering the world and the reality known before war is deeply confusing. One reality cannot be applied to the other. Rather than try to forget the experience of war, I think it more logical to understand that I have seen the broadest range of what humankind is capable of. It is real. But to stay locked in that dark time is to surrender the opportunity to enjoy life as it continues. I accept as truth that I do not control the experiences that come my way, but I do control the responses. And in controlling the responses, I take control of my life. I feel I become a free spirit in whether or not to choose anger, hatred, guilt or shame - who wants those feelings inside? To understand that the world is not perfect is to understand that I am not perfect and let forgiveness take its place in my vocabulary and arsenal of responses.

And I cannot let the activities of humans blind me to the greater beauty of all life. When I became anxious to receive treatment for this condition of PTSD, I realized how I had, over the years, created mental and physical responses used to preoccupy my mind to keep it from thinking of my time at war. Twitching eyebrows, chattering teeth, twitching muscles, tapping my fingers in specific sequence or numbers, counting stairs, memorizing written signs were frustrating activities to keep intrusive, unwanted thoughts away. To accept the truth is to help quiet the anxiety.

One day I was looking out a window across an empty farm field and spotted a beautiful stand of trees. From somewhere the remembrance of botany class flooded my thoughts. I stared at those trees thinking of the process of photosynthesis and the cycle of respiration. I thought of how green plants take the carbon dioxide that we exhale, mix it with water and glucose from sunlight, and produce oxygen that we then inhale to stay alive. As I stared, I imagined that the gases had colors: carbon dioxide was red and oxygen green; that I could see the red gases from the mouths of animals absorbed by the trees as they gave off the life giving green gases that humans inhaled. Though these colors do not exist, the gases and process do, and I was struck by the idea that I was part of something so much bigger than human life. I recalled my beautiful memories of the Pygmies and their connection and respect of life, the Africans and their ability to live so much as part of life, even holding ceremonies to honor the insects that protect the forest. I remembered the many times I stood in awe of the animal life and physical world in Africa. I realized that I had myself caught up in a world where the rules of human life were given more regard than the idea of belonging to something much larger and more beautiful. But here was proof that I belonged to life - all life - just by being alive and breathing.

This experience was highly important in offering relief to my soul and allowed me to see that it was not about human life but something much larger. I could choose to make it better or make it worse. But now I had to realize that I genuinely saw the beauty of all life, learned to respect all life. I had seen life as imperfect and learned to forgive and now having proof that I belonged to all life, it only made sense that I respect my life and forgive myself as part of that life; that I must let go of part of my ego and be part of the larger ego of life.

A short time later and by coincidence, I received a book titled A Treasury of Albert Schweitzer. Though known for and having received the Nobel Peace Prize for his writings on reverence for life, I was stunned to read a phrase that froze my mind and fixed on it: "I am life which wills to live, in the midst of life which wills to live... Only in the thinking man has the will-to-live become conscious of other will-to-live." Nothing could have hit more directly and exposed the most profound darkness of my soul. Schweitzer's writing continues, "The world, however, offers us the horrible drama of the will-to-live divided against itself. One existence holds its own at the cost of another: one destroys another."

I realized that the guilt and shame of war had just been identified. It was putting my will-to-live above the will-to-live of others. Call it what you want, I think this is a self-evident thought that just needed to be revealed and identified. I believe it also explained the rage for having been put in a position to have to make this decision, the rage at the energy needed over a long period of time to protect that will-to-live. Again my disbelief in what humans do to each other arose. But I cannot go back and try to employ what I know now into decisions made at that time. I can only forgive myself again for having that instinct to live and having put it in conflict with others' equally important will-to-live. It is real and what humans do; I am human and must know the truth in myself, in my soul. And maybe this is why the materialistic world will never hold the answers for me and why by that same self-evident thinking I do not search that world for answers.

Again I think of Africa and how I cannot explain how President Bokassa, Idi Amin, Shah of Iran, Macias Nguema, Baby Doc Duvalier and various other leaders tortured and slaughtered their own countrymen and close family members. Yet, when confronted, each cowardly fled. They very much understood the will-to-live in themselves but had the crippling inability to extend this to other lives. I, like many others, do not have this inability to extend the will-to-live to other life. I find this one of the principal differences that impacts the lives and deaths of people in the world today, especially veterans of war.

Finally, it cannot escape my thoughts that at war the pure energy we put into staying alive and to preserve the will-to-live must be expressed by a respect for life now. We must consider a use of that life to grow, become spiritually fulfilled, and make life better, if only for our individual selves and families. To have fought to stay alive only to return home and choose to stay in the darkness of that time at war makes no sense; it is not the result for which we fought. All veterans should have the opportunity to share that he or she has seen and experienced the greatest truth of what humans can survive, and we should be honored to have experienced that truth. We can put away in our soul that which needs to be put away, which has no value to hold onto, and respect the simple idea that we have been given life and go on and live it. In this we can be proud and extremely grateful. And because we returned home and have lives to live, maybe it is a good idea to live just a bit each day for those who were not as fortunate.

Coming in 2014
Look for my new books on Combat / Military PTSD
also Redefining PTSD, A Definition We Can Understand
and Resolutions That Make Sense.

And follow continuing updates on my website
www.michaelorban.com
or
www.mikeorbanptsd.com

IMPORTANT INFORMATION

All veterans of the Iraq and Afghanistan war are entitled to two years of medical treatment. Don't suffer unnecessarily nor cause loved ones to suffer from concern. Every Veterans Administration has a contact person who can walk the veteran through the process necessary to receive these benefits. Please visit these websites for more information. They are good resources for families, friends and the general public.

www.ncptsd.va.gov
National Center for Post Traumatic Stress Disorder.
This site is an educational resource on PTSD and traumatic stress for veterans and also for mental health care providers, researchers and the general public.

www.va.gov/rcs/
Readjustment Counseling Services (Vets Centers)
For war-zone veterans, Vets Centers offer superb counseling services at no cost AND provide services to wives and dependents as well. These services are offered to veterans of all conflicts.

Dr. Patti Levin
www.drpattilevin.com
Dr. Levin is a clinical psychologist who works with adults having anxiety disorders and has vast experience with victims of PTSD. An extremely informative web site.

VA Suicide Hotline
1.800.273.TALK (8255)
For help with all veteran and families issues on Combat Readjustment, COS, PTSD, PTS

COMMON RESPONSES TO TRAUMA AND COPING STRATEGIES

After a trauma, people may go though a wide range of normal responses. Such reactions may be experienced not only by people who experienced the trauma first-hand, but by those who have witnessed or heard about the trauma, or been involved with those immediately affected. Many reactions can be triggered by persons, places, or things associated with the trauma. Some reactions may appear totally unrelated. Here is a list of common physical and emotional reactions to trauma, as well as a list of helpful coping strategies. These are NORMAL reactions to ABNORMAL events.

PHYSICAL REACTIONS

- aches and pains like headaches, backaches, stomach aches

- sudden sweating and/or heart palpitations (fluttering)

- changes in sleep patterns, appetite, interest in sex

- constipation or diarrhea

- easily startled by noises or unexpected touch

- more susceptible to colds and illnesses

- increased use of alcohol or drugs and/or overeating

EMOTIONAL REACTIONS

- shock and disbelief

- fear and/or anxiety

- grief, disorientation, denial
- hyper-alertness or hyper vigilance
- irritability, restlessness, outbursts of anger or rage
- emotional swings -- like crying and then laughing
- worrying or ruminating -- intrusive thoughts of the trauma
- nightmares
- flashbacks -- feeling like the trauma is happening now
- feelings of helplessness, panic, feeling out of control
- increased need to control everyday experiences
- minimizing the experience
- attempts to avoid anything associated with trauma
- tendency to isolate oneself
- feelings of detachment
- concern over burdening others with problems
- emotional numbing or restricted range of feelings
- difficulty trusting and/or feelings of betrayal
- difficulty concentrating or remembering
- feelings of self-blame and/or survivor guilt
- shame
- diminished interest in everyday activities or depression
- unpleasant past memories resurfacing
- loss of a sense of order or fairness in the world; expectation of doom and fear of the future

HELPFUL COPING STRATEGIES

- mobilize a support system – reach out and connect with others, especially those who may have shared the stressful event
- talk about the traumatic experience with empathic listeners
- cry
- hard exercise like jogging, aerobics, bicycling, walking
- relaxation exercise like yoga, stretching, massage
- humor
- prayer and/ or meditation; listening to relaxing guided imagery; progressive deep muscle relaxation
- hot baths
- music and art
- maintain balanced diet and sleep cycle as much as possible
- avoid overusing stimulants like caffeine, sugar, or nicotine
- commitment to something personally meaningful and important every day
- hug those you love, pets included
- eat warm turkey, boiled onions, baked potatoes, cream-based soups – these are tryptophane activators, which help you feel tired but good (like after Thanksgiving dinner)
- proactive responses toward personal and community safety – organize or do something socially active
- write about your experience – in detail, just for yourself or to share with others

People are usually surprised that reactions to trauma can last longer than they expected. It may take weeks, months, and in some cases, many years to fully regain equilibrium. Many people will get through this period with the help and support of family and friends. But sometimes friends and family may push people to "get over it" before they're ready. Let them know that such responses are not helpful for you right now, though you appreciate that they are trying to help. Many people find that individual, group, or family counseling is helpful. These are some particular therapies that seem very helpful: EMDR (Eye Movement Desensitization and

Reprocessing) and EFT (Emotional Freedom Techniques) are phenomenally rapid and wonderful therapeutic methods. The key word for all these strategies is CONNECTION – ask for help, support, understanding, and opportunities to talk.

The Chinese character for crisis is a combination of two words - danger and opportunity. People who fully engage in recovery from trauma discover unexpected benefits. As they gradually heal their wounds, survivors find that they are also developing inner strength, compassion for others, increasing self-awareness, and often the most surprising -- a greater ability to experience joy and serenity than ever before.

UNDERSTANDING AND EDUCATION THAT HELPS MY OWN COMBAT READJUSTMENT

Over a period of several years I have developed several graphic models on Combat Readjustment. These models have helped in my personal struggle with combat readjustment (COS, PTSD).

These models illustrate a course of understanding growth in life beginning with our learned primary values through a traumatic event, reactions to that event and a path of hope and resolution. These models also show how we may become trapped in a painful psychological and spiritual darkness caused by that traumatic event. Visual representations provide a simple yet dynamic visual aid to understanding our individual state of mind and soul. By applying the reactions to an event, these models will provide a clear course of actions to take. The focus is to understand our reactions to a trauma as it relates to our elemental values and expectations.

The models then show how to resolve those reactions and transform life based on total experience. These models emphasize taking personal control of our lives, fearless desire to confront our experience and the reactions to that experience. Most importantly to see that there is hope and a path toward personal inner peace.

On the right are two models on Combat Readjustment. By applying 26 common reactions to a trauma, these models show how to understand those reactions and provide resolutions. For further details on how to use these models please contact me through my website at www.michaelorban.com A video presentation is also available.

Orban Life Integration & Transformation (OLIT)

Combat Model 1
Post-Combat Readjustment COS/PTS/PTSD

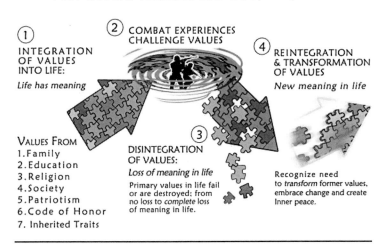

(1) INTEGRATION OF VALUES INTO LIFE:

Life has meaning

(2) COMBAT EXPERIENCES CHALLENGE VALUES

(4) REINTEGRATION & TRANSFORMATION OF VALUES

New meaning in life

VALUES FROM
1. Family
2. Education
3. Religion
4. Society
5. Patriotism
6. Code of Honor
7. Inherited Traits

(3) DISINTEGRATION OF VALUES:

Loss of meaning in life

Primary values in life fail or are destroyed; from no loss to *complete* loss of meaning in life.

Recognize need to *transform* former values, embrace change and create Inner peace.

Combat Model 1B
Severe Confrontation with Values & Event

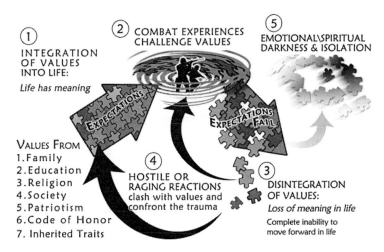

(1) INTEGRATION OF VALUES INTO LIFE:

Life has meaning

(2) COMBAT EXPERIENCES CHALLENGE VALUES

(5) EMOTIONAL\SPIRITUAL DARKNESS & ISOLATION

EXPECTATIONS

EXPECTATIONS FAIL

VALUES FROM
1. Family
2. Education
3. Religion
4. Society
5. Patriotism
6. Code of Honor
7. Inherited Traits

(4) HOSTILE OR RAGING REACTIONS clash with values and confront the trauma

(3) DISINTEGRATION OF VALUES:

Loss of meaning in life

Complete inability to move forward in life

THE MODELS WORK: A Testimonial

I have used these models in the following situations: 12 Christian adults working with chronic illnesses, a small group of persons developing a joy-filled life, a seminary seminar on "Pastoral Care of Veterans and their Families", army, navy and air force hospital chaplains, civilian hospital chaplains and several individuals with post traumatic stress disorders (PTSD). In each situation individuals were able to adapt the model to their experiences. These models provide a visual way for persons to develop meanings of their life struggles. Since we are visual persons, the models help us to take realistic steps for life-giving directions.

Chaplain Fred Shilling

ABOUT THE AUTHOR

Michael S. Orban was born in Wisconsin in 1950, the fourth oldest of ten in a Catholic middle class family. He enjoyed a safe, carefree life, never traveling more than eighty miles from home until drafted into the US Army in 1969. Serving in the Vietnam War, by the age of twenty-one he had flown over twenty-five combat assaults and earned the bronze star, air medal and combat infantryman's medal. He returned home in a spiritual darkness and began his journey of years traveling the world trying to retrieve his soul from that darkness.

He now resides in West Bend, Wisconsin, where he is a freelance writer and retired construction business owner. See Michael's website for information on his forthcoming book *When Eyes Die, The Stranger Arrives.*

www.michaelorban.com
262.247.2456